WEIGHT TRAINING

Kim Beckwith
University of Texas—Austin

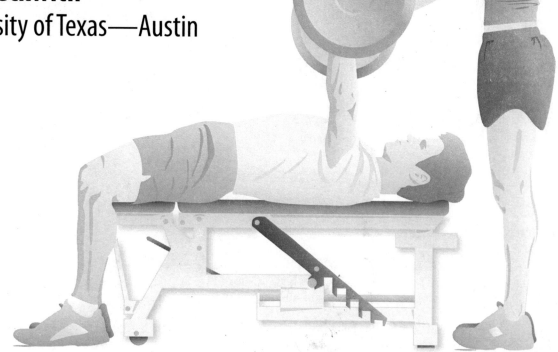

 KENDALL/HUNT PUBLISHING COMPANY
4050 Westmark Drive   Dubuque, Iowa 52002

Cover art credits:
Front cover weight © 2008, Yuri Arcurs
Back cover weight © 2008, Mark Stout Photography
Bulleye image © 2008, George Pappas
All used under license from Shutterstock, Inc.

ISBN 978-0-7575-5197-0

Printed in the United States of America
10   9   8   7   6   5   4

Contents

CHAPTER 1

Introduction and Let's Get Started!

Often when the word *strength* enters into a conversation, people think of men with bulging muscles or NFL football players crashing into one another on the field of battle. People then ask why ordinary individuals should give serious consideration to engaging in a strength training program. Sometimes people make statements such as, "What good will increased strength do for me in my business as a computer programmer?"

To answer these questions and dispel some of the misconceptions surrounding the topic of strength, let us consider what strength is and why strength can give everyone an advantage in participating in the activities of daily life.

STRENGTH AND ITS ADVANTAGES

Strength is defined as the ability to exert force against resistance. Force is the basis of all motion, and when we examine the world we live in, we can easily observe that it is a world of motion. Strength then becomes an important aspect in performing the tasks of daily living, such as lifting, walking, running, doing housework, and engaging in recreational tasks.

Another aspect of movement is *power*. Power is defined as the rate at which energy can be released, or the rate of doing work. The formula for power is as follows:

$$\text{Power} = \text{Force} \times \frac{\text{Displacement in the direction of force}}{\text{Time}}$$

Displacement in the direction of force divided by time equals velocity. Thus, the two factors that influence power are force (strength) and velocity. To affect power, a training program must affect either strength or velocity or, if possible, both of these factors at the same time. Of these two variables, it is much more difficult to bring about changes in velocity than in strength. Thus, the key to developing increased power is the change that a training program can bring about on the development of strength.

In this way, power becomes one of the keys to a more productive life. It is not time itself that is important but rather what takes place in that time; productivity determines the difference between success and failure. By increasing your power output, you can accomplish more work in a shorter period of time.

Consider the practical example of mowing the lawn. If you increase your strength and bring about a greater power output, the work of mowing the lawn can be accomplished much more quickly. A friend gave the following reason for participating in a strength program: "I can finish my yard work in a short period of time, and this allows me to get on the golf course where I can apply force to the golf ball with a great amount of joy!"

The past few years have seen some remarkable performances in athletic achievement. Athletes are jumping farther and higher, runners are breaking records in most of the running events, and swimming records are broken in nearly every large swimming meet.

Physiologically, the body has been operating the same way for a long while, so there must be a reason why the human body is breaking athletic records that were thought to be impossible to change. When we examine the training procedures these record-breaking athletes engage in, we find that one of the greatest causes of improvement is the proper use of a strength training program.

If strength is the ability to exert force and force is a tendency to cause motion, then strength is important not only to the athlete but also to all individuals in everyday life. If more work can be accomplished in a shorter period of time, a person is more powerful. If all else remains equal, an increase in strength will contribute to an improvement in the performance of the human body.

Another reason for engaging in strength training is that it makes you feel better and look better. A person does not have to be a so-called bodybuilder to value how an attractive body can have a positive effect on self-concept. In a survey of the men and women engaged in a series of strength development classes, over 80 percent responded that the major reason for taking the class was that they wished "to look better."

Since many people express a desire to look better, a discussion of body composition is important. The human body is composed of materials that are referred to as *lean body mass* and *fat mass*. Lean body mass is made up primarily of muscle tissue, connective tissue, bone, and fluids, and fat mass is the fat that the body stores. Many people in our society have an excess amount of body fat, and this leads to the problem of obesity. One estimate is that by the age of fifty, almost 50 percent of the people in the United States are approaching obesity, or overfatness.

The relationship between the amount of muscle mass in the body and excess body fat is often overlooked. The amount and size of muscle decrease in many people as they get older because of a lack of a strength training stimulus. As muscle mass decreases, the person uses less energy even at rest, and a greater percentage of the body weight becomes fat. Fat tissue does not burn nearly as many calories at rest as muscle tissue, and thus the individual continues to gain body fat. In other words, many people become fat because they are using fewer calories as a result of the loss of muscle mass caused by a lack of activity. Since people spend more time in sitting than in any other activity, the average American becomes overfat as he or she grows older.

Ancel Keys, a researcher in weight control, showed that the decrease in caloric expenditure in different age groups at rest was related to the change in muscle mass rather than to age. For example, at age sixty a person will use approximately fifteen calories less per hour than a person who is twenty-six years of age. Over a twenty-four-hour period this would be a total of 360 unused calories per day. If that person wanted to retain the same eating habits but not put on fat, he or she would have to walk approximately six miles each day to expend the 360 calories, since the energy used in walking one mile is about sixty calories. The sixty-year-old individual, therefore, must increase activity, decrease caloric intake, or else put on more fat.

A person can help eliminate the problem of overfatness by using a strength development program to maintain muscle mass so that caloric expenditure at rest won't decrease. Thus a person won't have to exercise so extensively to combat obesity. The body will continue to use more calories if muscle mass is maintained throughout life.

A common misconception about strength development is that a strength training program will cause "muscle-boundness," or a loss of flexibility. Many scientific studies indicate that the opposite is true—that engaging in a strength program correctly will actually bring about an improvement in flexibility. One study, conducted at the Olympic Games, tested the flexibility of the competing athletes and found that the most flexible athletes were the gymnasts, swimmers, and weightlifters.

The key to maintaining good flexibility is to take the body parts through a full range of motion. This can be accomplished by engaging in a proper strength development program. By using correct techniques, you will develop strength throughout the entire range of movement of the body musculature.

The ability of the body to resist the stresses that can result from an injury can be increased by obtaining a greater amount of strength. In the athletic world, statistics indicate that athletic injuries, such as in football, are reduced when teams engage in a strength development program. The fatigue of sports participation combats the body's ability to withstand the disruption of movement, but with an increase in strength, the athlete is more powerful and thus retains the ability to perform in the later stages of the contest. This same advantage is important in performing everyday tasks, such as lifting or carrying objects.

Health Benefits of Strength Training

Besides increasing strength, creating more collagenous fibrils in connective tissue, bringing about changes in nervous tissue, and increasing bone density, a strength training program has other health benefits.

Some of the risk factors for coronary heart disease (CHD) are determined by the variables of blood cholesterol and blood lipids and the transport molecules known as lipid proteins. A total body strength program has a positive effect on these variables.

High blood sugar (glucose) levels and high insulin levels are risk factors for diabetes and CHD. Recent evidence has revealed that strength training can bring about positive changes in glucose metabolism.

Colon cancer is associated with a prolonged gastrointestinal transit time, and sedentary living is associated with an increase of cancer of the colon. An accelerated transit time is associated with a strength training program that develops the abdominal musculature. One study found that strength training brought about an average acceleration of 56 percent in gastrointestinal transit time after thirteen weeks of training.

WOMEN AND STRENGTH TRAINING

Women considering strength training are sometimes concerned that strength exercises will make them appear less feminine. The fear is that training will produce large, unsightly, bulging muscles. In the past few years, research has disputed this myth. Women have the same muscle properties as men, but because of endocrinological differences, they respond to a training stimulus in different ways. Before puberty, there is little difference between the muscular size and strength of boys and girls, but with the onset of puberty, testosterone from the testes of the male and estrogen from the ovaries of the female begin to enter the bloodstream and trigger the development of the appropriate secondary sexual characteristics. The result is that men develop a greater quantity of muscle tissue and respond with a greater gain of muscle mass when they engage in a strength program.

In most cases, women will not gain a large amount of muscle mass when training, but they will obtain increased strength, which will enable them to better perform daily activities. The diameter of a muscle cell can increase as much as 30 percent without measurable growth in the girth of a body limb, so women do not have to worry about increased body size. There is no physiological reason for women not to engage in a strength training program and no need to suggest different training programs on the basis of sex. Both women and men can experience the same general benefits; it is only the degree of gain in muscle tissue that will differ.

STRENGTH TRAINING FOR THOSE OVER FORTY

Some people ask whether those over the age of forty should engage in strength training. The answer is that all the advantages of increased strength hold true for any age.

Research comparing the rate of strength gains in men and women of various ages shows that the rates are similar for all age groups. One study used men and women with an average age of ninety. After strength training for eight weeks in a three-day-per-week program, the subjects experienced a 174 percent increase in strength.

Our youth-oriented society tends to neglect the needs of its older citizens. If you are an individual who falls into the over-forty category, rest assured that engaging in a proper strength development program can not only increase your strength but also increase the overall performance of your body.

STRENGTH TRAINING AND CHILDREN

Another question involves whether strength training is an appropriate activity for children before the age of pubescence. At one time the assumption was that prepubescent boys and girls could not increase strength because of a lack of adult hormones. A large amount of research indicates that this assumption is false and that children can obtain significant strength gains in a properly designed program.

Other research has revealed that a strength training program will also contribute to motor performance gains and other health-related benefits such as injury prevention, improvements in blood lipid profiles, an increase in bone density, and a positive effect on body composition. Strength training also has been found to contribute to a more positive self-concept and body image in children.

The National Strength and Conditioning Association and the American Orthopaedic Society for Sports Medicine have stated that proper strength training will have lasting benefits on young participants. They have suggested the following guidelines in the design of strength programs for this age group:

1. Require a medical examination before participating in the strength program.
2. Make sure the training facility provides a safe exercise environment.
3. Participants should have the emotional maturity to accept and follow proper training directions.
4. Instructors should be qualified and remember the uniqueness of each child.
5. Include warm-up and cool-down exercises in the training program.
6. Demonstrate proper exercise techniques for each exercise utilized in the program.
7. Increase the resistance gradually as strength improves in the participants.
8. Prohibit one repetition maximum lifts during the program to prevent possible injury.
9. Remember that strength training is part of an overall conditioning program.

These guidelines are excellent suggestions not only for children but also for any strength trainer regardless of age.

CONCLUSION

An examination of all the ways strength can contribute to the overall efficiency of the human body reveals that a strength development program should be a lifetime process. When you make the decision to start a strength program, you have started a new lifestyle. Maintaining that lifestyle is important, since strength is reversible and will decline if you do not continue to obtain a strength stimulus for your entire life.

MOVEMENT PREP

If you've had any experience in sports or training, you've probably done some stretching. We're told from a young age that we need to stretch in order to prevent injury. Stretching is viewed as a precursor to working out, just as brushing your teeth is a precursor to going to bed. Not surprisingly, most people approach stretching routines halfheartedly.

There's tremendous value in traditional stretch-and-hold, or "static," stretching if executed properly, and it's part of the Core Workout—but only when done *after* a workout. After all, a warm rubber band stretches a lot farther than a cold one, right? So it's best to stretch when the body is warm, which it is after training. (We'll touch more on this in the Regeneration section of the workout.)

We've replaced preworkout static stretching with a Movement Preparation series of exercises that's an essential part of your routine, not just a necessary evil like stretching. In fact, if you were to incorporate just one element of this book into your existing workout routine, I'd want it to be Movement Prep. Nothing else provides so much value in so little time.

Movement Prep, as the term suggests, prepares the body for movement. It boosts heart rate, blood flow to the muscles, and core temperature. It also improves the function of the nervous system.

Think of the Movement Prep routine as taking a few minutes to warm up a car that has been sitting outside in cold temperatures all night. It also can be compared to a pilot's turning on all the switches in the cockpit before a flight. If you go through this checklist, you'll be dialed in physically and mentally for the rest of your workout. The end result will be a significant improvement in mobility, flexibility, and stability, on top of an increase of speed and power output by nearly 20 percent compared to static stretching.

We want to improve the long-term mobility and flexibility of muscles. Rather than have them stretch and go back to where they were—as is the case with traditional stretching—we want your body to remember those ranges of motion.

We do this through a process of lengthening the muscle (known as active elongation), which is no different from a traditional stretch. But then comes the crucial difference: After you stretch the muscle to this new range of motion, you contract the muscle. In other words, you don't just stretch the muscle and then end the stretch. You actually use it in that stretched position.

That does a couple of useful things. First, by strengthening muscles in that new range of motion, you stabilize all the tiny muscles around your joints that help hold the joints together. That will improve posture and performance and decrease the potential for injury. Second, and most important, we're going to "activate" these little muscles, throwing on the light switches so they're available and participating all the time.

Nearly all of the athletes we see for the first time have at least one muscle group that's completely shut off. This can cause other areas of the body to compensate, which ultimately leads to injury. An example of this would be one of the small muscles of the hips, the gluteus medius, which if not activated will lead to lower-back problems, knee pain, and groin strain. It's as if someone flipped the circuit breaker, cutting off the power to these little muscles.

And that's in elite athletes. Think of how many switches the average adult has deactivated, considering he rarely does anything more challenging than walking up or down stairs.

Thankfully, with Movement Prep, it takes only a day or two to reactivate these inactive areas. These 10 exercises, which require no equipment, enable your body to recall those movements that perhaps haven't been used since childhood. (If you are a young athlete, Movement Prep is going to make sure that you maintain the ability to perform these movements.)

Another difference between traditional stretching and Movement Prep is that the goal of the former is to relax muscles, to allow you to get into a stretched position and hold it. In Movement Prep, you're going to contract your muscles, which is to say you will be activating them by squeezing them.

Let's take your butt, which we prefer to call your gluteus maximus and usually shorten to "glutes." Take a moment and squeeze your left butt cheek, then your right. Pretty simple, right? Yet most people, even active athletes, rarely activate their glutes. As a result, they never take full advantage of these tremendously powerful muscles that should be a big part of everyday movement.

Instead, we spend most of our time sitting on our glutes, which causes the muscles opposite them—the hip flexors—to become tight and inactive. The neuromuscular relationship of these opposing muscle groups is known as *reciprocal inhibition,* which is a fancy way of saying that when one muscle group contracts, the other relaxes. When one fires, the other reloads. Movement Prep is reciprocal inhibition at work.

The Movement Prep routine wakes these muscles up—and not just for your workout. They'll remain switched on for the rest of the day. Here's why that's important: Let's say you're walking on a winter day, and your foot slips on some ice. How well your body reacts to that slip on the ice depends on your *proprioception,* the system of pressure sensors in the joints, muscles, and tendons that your body uses to maintain balance. Movement Prep, in switching on your body's small muscles, also tunes your sense of proprioception. It prepares your body for random, chaotic movement by fine-tuning its nerves and feedback mechanisms.

We'll generally do 5 to 10 repetitions of each of the Movement Prep exercises; not only will it feel like part of your workout (as opposed to a boring precursor to the real thing), at first it might feel like a workout itself. But don't worry: Your body will quickly condition itself to the exercises, and when you're done, you'll feel warmed up, rather than worn down. And you'll be better prepared for whatever follows, whether it's a workout, a game, or just the normal actions of everyday life.

Summary: Movement Prep is going to increase your core temperature and elongate your muscles actively so that you make long-term flexibility gains. It will improve your balance and proprioception, and it is the perfect formula for building mobility, flexibility, stability, and strength.

Time Capsule: Movement Prep requires no equipment and a minimum investment of time. I've provided different versions of the Core Workout to fit any lifestyle or level of training, but you'll find that Movement Prep is a common denominator. If you were to do nothing else, I would want you to commit to mastering and performing the Movement Prep routine two to six times a week, if only for 10 minutes. It provides a tremendous return for a minimum investment.

The following pages provide a look at the Movement Prep exercises. As with any new exercises, the pictures will help you better understand the movement. The selection and repetitions of each exercise will vary depending on the training goals for that particular day, week, and 3-week segment of the Core Workout, which are outlined in the full Core Workout worksheets.

A CD-ROM featuring video of these exercises is available at www.coreperformance.com. (Verstegen)

HIP CROSSOVER

Unit:

Movement Prep.

Objective:

To build mobility and strength in your torso by disassociating hips and shoulders.

Starting Position:

Lie supine (faceup) on the floor, arms and shoulders extended out at your sides and flat, feet flat on the floor.

Procedure:

Twist your bent legs to the right until they reach the floor, then twist to the left.

Coaching Key(s):

Keep your abs drawn in and shoulders, torso, and feet in contact with the ground.

You Should Feel:

Stretching and contracting of your core muscles.

Progression:

Try this move with your hips and knees bent 90 degrees and your feet off the ground.

Second Progression:

Perform this move with your legs straight.

SCORPION

Unit:

Movement Prep.

Objective:

To lengthen and strengthen the muscles of your core; stretch your chest, quads, hips, and abs; and activate your glutes.

Starting Position:

Lie prone (belly-down) on the floor, with your arms and shoulders pinned in the "spread 'em!" pose.

Procedure:

Thrust your left heel toward your right hand by firing your left glute while keeping your right hip glued to the ground. Alternate legs.

Coaching Key(s):

Be sure to fire (squeeze) your glute as you thrust your heel.

You Should Feel:

A stretch in your quads and hip flexors, along with activation of your glutes.

CALF STRETCH

Unit:

Movement Prep.

Objective:

To increase flexibility in this very often-neglected area.

Starting Position:

From the pushup position, place your left foot over your right heel. Your weight should be on the ball of your right foot.

Procedure:

Pull your right toes up toward your shin while you push your right heel down toward the ground with your left foot. Exhale as you lower your heel. Hold for a one count, raise your right heel again, and repeat.

Coaching Key(s):

You're pulling your toes up toward the shin at the same time you're pushing the heel to the ground. Then push back through the new range of motion.

You Should Feel:

A stretch in your calf and ankle.

Progression:

Bend the knee of your working leg to shift the emphasis to your Achilles tendon.

HAND WALK
a.k.a. *"World's Second-Greatest Stretch"*

Unit:

Movement Prep.

Objective:

To build stability in your shoulders and core and to lengthen your hamstrings, calves, and lower-back muscles.

Starting Position:

Stand with your legs straight and hands on floor.

Procedure:

Keeping your legs straight and belly button drawn in, walk your hands out. Still keeping your legs straight, walk your feet back up to your hands.

Coaching Key(s):

Use short "ankle steps" to walk back up to your hands. That is, take baby steps using only your ankles—don't use your knees, hips, or quads.

You Should Feel:

A stretch in your hamstrings, lower back, glutes, and calves and a burning in the fronts of your shins.

INVERTED HAMSTRING

Unit:

Movement Prep.

Objective:

To improve hamstring flexibility and balance, along with dynamic pillar stabilization.

Starting Position:

Balance on your right foot with perfect posture (tummy tight, shoulders back and down).

Procedure:

Bending at the waist, and maintaining perfect posture, grab your right foot with your left hand, extending your left leg back as you fire the left glute. (You might find it easier to extend forward with both hands out, as shown, rather than while grabbing a foot.) Your shoulder and heel should move as one, forming a straight line. Take a step back at the end of each rep as you alternate legs.

Coaching Key(s):

Your body should be in a straight line from ear to ankle. Keep your back and pelvis flat! Someone should be able to place a broomstick snugly across your back.

You Should Feel:

A stretch in your hamstrings.

LATERAL LUNGE

Unit:

Movement Prep.

Objective:

To open up the muscles of your groin and hips. Also to hold pillar strength as you sit back and down.

Starting Position:

Stand with perfect posture.

Procedure:

Step out to the right, keeping your toes pointed straight ahead and feet flat. Squat by sitting back and down onto your right leg, keeping your left leg straight and the weight on the right leg's mid-foot to heel. Squat as low as possible, keeping your left leg straight and holding this position for 2 seconds. Return to the standing position and repeat.

Coaching Key(s):

Keep your feet pointed straight ahead and flat throughout.

You Should Feel:

A stretch in the inside of your thigh.

FORWARD LUNGE/FOREARM-TO-INSTEP a.k.a. *"World's Greatest Stretch"*

Unit:

Movement Prep.

Objective:

To improve flexibility in your hips, hamstrings, lower back, torso, groin, hip flexors, and quads.

Starting Position:

Take a large step forward with your left leg, as if doing a lunge. Place and support weight on your right hand, even with your left foot.

Procedure:

Take your left elbow and reach down to your instep (forward leg) while keeping your back knee off the ground. Then move your left hand outside your left foot and push your hips straight to the sky, pulling your toe up toward your shin. Finally, step forward into the next lunge.

Coaching Key(s):

Keep your back knee off the ground. Exhale as you reach your elbow to the floor. At the end, make sure both hands remain in contact with the ground as you lift your hips and pull your toe toward the shin.

You Should Feel:

A stretch in your groin, your back leg's hip flexor, and your front leg's glute. During the second part, you should feel a stretch in your front leg's hamstring and calf.

BACKWARD LUNGE WITH A TWIST

Unit:

Movement Prep.

Objective:

To lengthen your hip flexors, quads, and core. This stretches everything from your big toes to your hands.

Starting Position:

With your feet together, step back with your right leg into a lunge.

Procedure:

Arch your back slightly while twisting your torso over your left leg and while reaching your right hand to the sky. Push back and out of that position into the next lunge.

Coaching Key(s):

As you lean back and rotate, fire (squeeze) the glute of your back leg. This creates reciprocal inhibition, lengthening your hip flexors.

You Should Feel:

A stretch from your back leg through your core and lats, and a stretch of your hip flexors.

DROP LUNGE

Unit:

Movement Prep.

Objective:

To improve flexibility in your hips, glutes, and iliotibial (IT) bands—thick bands of tissue in either leg that extend from the thigh down over the outside of the knee and attach to the tibia (the larger lower-leg bone).

Starting Position:

Stand balanced with your arms extended.

Procedure:

Turn your hips to the left and reach back with your left foot until it's about 2 feet to the outside of your right foot, your left toes pointing to your right heel. Rotate your hips back so they're facing forward again and square with your shoulders and feet. You want your chest up and tummy tight, and the majority of your weight on your right leg. Drop into a full squat by pushing your hips back and down, keeping your right heel on the ground. Now drive hard off your right leg, standing back up, and repeat, moving to your right for the allotted number of reps. Switch legs. Return to the left.

Coaching Key(s):

Turn your hips to drop your leg behind. Keep your toes pointed straight, with the back toe to the front heel.

You Should Feel:

A stretch in your hips, glutes, and IT bands.

SUMO SQUAT-TO-STAND

Unit:

Movement Prep.

Objective:

To improve flexibility in your hamstrings, groin, ankles, and lower back.

Starting Position:

Stand tall, with your feet outside your hips.

Procedure:

Bend at the waist, grabbing under your big toes. Keeping your arms straight and inside your knees, pull your hips down until they're between your ankles, and lift your chest up. Then tuck your chin and try to straighten your legs, holding on to your toes as you straighten out your hips and knees.

Coaching Key(s):

Hold on to your toes at the bottom of the movement. Pull your chest up and your shoulders back and down, and try to drive your hips forward to get your torso vertical, not horizontal. As you lift your hips, keep your back flat.

You Should Feel:

A stretch in your groin, glutes, lower back, and, to a lesser degree, ankles. (Verstegen)

CHAPTER 2

Periodization

"Periodization" is the scientific community's name for weight training in a cycle of increasing intensity and decreasing volume, with the cycle being made up of several distinct *periods.* It's important that you understand periodization because research has shown this method of weight work to be the most result-producing way a person can train. In other words, we're not telling you to train using the periodization model because *we* train that way but because study after research study has concluded that this method of training produces more positive physical results—more strength, more power, and more lean body weight—than any other method known. If this book can be said to have a central truth, this is it. Periodization is the best way to train.

We know, of course, that few of you are interested in really concentrating on the production of maximum strength. Neither, any longer, are we. And, while periodization can clearly be used to create great, even *incredible* strength gains, we suggest this method to you because it is also the best weight-training method to increase your level of fitness in every way. Used properly, it will make you more flexible, more enduring, more fit cardiovascularly, and—as an added plus—it is more interesting than other methods of training.

The psychological benefits of periodization training alone would sell us on it as a training method, since the worst thing that can happen to a would-be trainer is to get started on a program that's always the same. Boredom kills more fitness programs than any other villain—more than injuries, more than lack of time, more than lack of equipment. People get tired of doing the same things all the time, whether it's working on an assembly line or running laps around a small indoor track. The advantage of periodization is that no two workouts are ever the same. Every day you'll either vary the exercises, the poundage, or the number of repetitions so that you have different things to think about, different "goals." Periodization has a built-in reward system. By increasing your training poundages gradually, you condition yourself to succeed and your self-confidence will grow. In time, this will allow you to make weight training a permanent part of your life, a part that will pay dividends as long as you live.

Terry: "In the early sixties, when I was beginning to consider myself a 'weightlifter,' I used to read and try everything I could get my hands on about how to train. When *Strength and Health* magazine began talking about isometric contraction, my training partners and I all tried isometric contraction; when Paul Anderson said the secret to strength lay in partial movements, we all did partial movements; when someone wrote in *Iron Man* magazine that the key was high repetition work, we all did lots of high reps. We tried, in other words, *everything,* looking for the talisman that would give us strength and size and, we hoped, a national title. And while my buddies and I were training in Austin— and learning from our training—other athletes were doing the same thing. And eventually, through trial and error, we found and shared systems that seemed to work. The system we finally hit upon was a crude form of cycle training, and it involved using a variety of repetitions and weights rather than repeating a set number of repetitions day after day.

"While athletes here in the United States were using trial and error methods to achieve optimal performance, U.S. sports scientists began research studies in an effort to determine which combination of sets and repetitions created the greatest gains in strength. In 1962, Dr. Richard Berger published an article in *Research Quarterly* stating that he felt the optimal routine for developing strength was 3 sets of 6 repetitions per exercise, 3 times per week. Then, in 1966, Dr. Patrick O'Shea strengthened Berger's claims with another study that again found that 3 sets of 6 produced the greatest short-term gains. However, despite the laboratory evidence, most advanced weightlifters from the mid-sixties on didn't train year-round using 3 sets of 6 reps. What the athletes of this era had discovered was that no matter how much they *wanted* to train 'heavy' all the time, their bodies and minds wouldn't allow them to do it.

"There were some guys around who worked to their limit either on reps or singles all the time in their training, but they didn't last long. They either burned out or got an injury of some sort. Those of us who lasted and continued to improve found that we had to start out conservatively—to use light weights for a while and then go on to the increasingly heavier poundages. Then, following a meet, we'd always take a break before coming back to begin again with light weights."

To best understand how periodization came about, we must journey to the Soviet Union—home of the world's strongest men and women and home of Dmitri Matveyev, a renowned sports scientist. For years, Matveyev studied hundreds of world-class athletes from a variety of sports to ascertain which training systems created the best gains. He looked at not just a normal eight- to ten-week precontest preparation period but at the entire year. He found that most world-class athletes trained so that they used "high volume–low intensity" training in the early part of their "cycle," then switched to "low volume–high intensity" work. He called this training method "periodization." A Russian weightlifter, for example, would do several sets of high repetitions (repetitions representing volume—in other words, the higher the repetitions the higher the volume of work) with relatively light weights (weights representing intensity—the lighter the weight in any given exercise, the lower the intensity of the work being done). This high volume (high repetitions)–low intensity (light weights) pattern would be followed during the first period of the weightlifter's training cycle. Then, in the next period of the training cycle, the trainer would switch to fewer repetitions (lower volume) and heavier weights (higher intensity) as his cycle drew to an end.

There are some who cite Matveyev's work as one of the reasons for the advances made by Soviet athletes during the 1960s, when, in sports such as weightlifting, for instance, they dramatically outdistanced their American counterparts. In any case, Matveyev's model of training didn't really enter the American sports bloodstream until the mid-1970s, and even now most American athletes who train with weights use either a rather crude form of periodization based mostly on intuition and past successes or some other method of training altogether.

Matveyev's theories of periodization, it should be noted, were based on his observation of the many, many world-class athletes who were already *using* periodization long before Matveyev "discovered" it. But his formalization of the theory was quickly applied by the Soviet sports establishment, which exerts considerable control over the training practices of their athletes. We do know that some Soviet athletes were using extremely sophisticated periodization systems well before the full explanation of Matveyev's findings had hit the United States.

Matveyev's findings corroborated in the world of sports those of the eminent Canadian scientist Dr. Hans Selye, who, through his own experiments and observations, formulated what is called the General Adaptation Syndrome. Selye feels that there are three levels, or phases, of adaptation that people undergo when they begin to exercise. The initial phase, the "alarm stage," is characterized by stiffness and muscle soreness, especially if the trainer hasn't been involved in any sort of exercise program for some time. The second phase, "resistance," is the development of a greater training capacity, or "fitness," as the body accustoms itself to the demands of the exercise and prepares itself to move on to higher levels. The third phase, "overtraining," or fatigue, is caused by training too hard or too long without adequate rest periods.

Periodization is successful because it allows the body to gradually adapt to the stress of exercise. Also, some 1978 research done by Morehouse and Miller suggests that the high volume–low intensity training that constitutes the beginning phase of periodization creates maximum muscular hypertrophy (muscular enlargement), which is important because other research has shown that larger muscles have a greater capacity to gain in strength. Morehouse and Miller's research further suggests that the best way to achieve muscular hypertrophy is to use 3 to 5 sets with between 8 and 20 repetitions per set, a suggestion that has been borne out by subsequent studies.

Within the past several years, numerous research projects have been completed that compare periodization training to the more traditional 3-sets-of-6 approach and to other popular training methods. Much of this work has been done by Dr. Mike Stone, who has consistently found that periodization trainers make better progress than those using other methods. In particular, the gains made in hip and leg strength through periodization were exceptional compared to other methods of training. Studies by Stone, and sometimes by us, have been done on Olympic weightlifters, a women's softball team, football teams, teenagers, children, middle-aged men and women, and several groups of "average" students enrolled in university weight-training classes, and *all* have shown that the periodization approach produces the greatest gains.

Jan: "I used a periodization approach to powerlifting almost from the beginning. And as we've come to understand more of the physiological underpinnings for periodization's success, I've adapted my workouts more closely to what research now tells us will create the greatest gains in performance. It seems to have worked." We've also encouraged the members of our powerlifting team here at UT to train according to these methods and those who've stuck with the system have made remarkable gains, often becoming national and world champions. Judy Gedney attributes much of her success to the periodization approach she has used for the past two years. Indeed, more and more of the top powerlifters and Olympic lifters now in the United States are using or switching to some form of periodization.

In short, periodization works. But those of you whose desires run more toward fitness and fun than toward competition and conquest may be wondering why you need to be concerned with such seemingly complicated planning for your workouts. Well, first of all, if you're going to invest both time and money in a new fitness program, you deserve to get something back that's really worthwhile. Naturally, doing *anything*—if you've been doing nothing—is a step in the right direction, but you deserve more than just a step for your efforts. You deserve to *arrive*. Periodization will allow you not only to start but also to arrive. The form of periodization we recommend has four basic parts:

1. Hypertrophy: High Volume—Low Intensity

The Hypertrophy (muscle increase) phase is designed to allow the lifter to adapt physiologically so that he or she is better able, when the time comes later in the cycle, to perform at higher levels of intensity. Three to five sets of ten repetitions are used in each exercise. Besides the increase in lean muscle weight that the Hypertrophy phase brings, another benefit is the building of short-term endurance (anaerobic capacity). This increased anaerobic activity will combat fatigue during the higher intensity work that follows.

One thing to remember about the Hypertrophy stage of training is that you should not expect to make large increases in strength at this time. The purpose of this first stage of training is to prepare you to make large gains in strength later in the cycle, *after* your body has adapted to the program through Hypertrophy and an increased anaerobic capacity. That's why when the second stage, called Basic Strength, is reached, your strength should increase more rapidly. In your Hypertrophy training, concentrate on using good speed and weights heavy enough so that you feel as if you've really worked out. But don't worry if you can't add much extra weight. Try to increase the weights slightly each week, of course, but be careful not to add so much that you can't do the required number of repetitions.

2. Basic Strength: Moderate Volume—Medium Intensity

The Basic Strength phase is characterized by 3 to 5 sets of 5 repetitions per exercise with increasingly heavy weights. Here, it's important that you set goal, or target, weights for yourself each week in all your exercises and that you do your best to attain those weights (see pages 27 and 28). Basic Strength is an intermediate stage between the light weights of Hypertrophy and the heavy weights of the Power phase. Basic Strength allows both the body and mind to adapt to the greater weights to come.

3. Power: Low Volume—High Intensity

In the Power stage, the decreased volume—3 to 5 sets of 2 or 3 repetitions—allows the body to be even less fatigued, though heavier weights are being lifted. This means that as you concentrate more on explosive power, you'll be able to lift heavier weights. During this phase, emphasis should be placed on the technique of the lifts and the speed with which the weights are moved. If you're doing squats, for instance, control the weight on the way down but then explode upward, moving the weight as rapidly as possible without jumping off the floor at the top. (In all your exercises, move the weight as rapidly as possible while still using good form, even though you're using heavier weights.) This high-intensity training is believed to have a positive effect on the central nervous system. By concentrating on the speed of the lifts, the nerves are trained to send the right patterns of neural orders to the muscles so that they perform explosively.

It is still important in this stage of your training, however, that you not miss any of the repetitions with the heavier weights—not a single rep. While more research needs to be done in this area, it appears that you can train yourself to fail just as you can train yourself to succeed. Choosing weights that are too heavy is not only dangerous but it teaches the central nervous system to give way rather than fight through. It conditions you to fail, making subsequent failure easier. It can also create a fear of heavy poundages.

Once the Power phase is completed, a weightlifter, for instance, would enter a competition. A football player, however, facing a long season, would go on a *maintenance* program to keep as much of his strength and power for as long as possible during the season. It's generally felt that athletes with extended seasons should train with weights at least twice a week and use only 3 sets of between 3 and 5 repetitions per set in order to maintain their strength level and to avoid staleness and overtraining.

4. Rejuvenation: Very Low Volume—Very Low Intensity

The Rejuvenation, or Active Rest phase, is simply a time for you to let your physical and mental well fill up again. This is a time for racquetball, hiking, cycling, and trying out new exercises with the weights. Rejuvenation can last for as little as a week or up to a month depending on the physiological and emotional needs of the trainer. This phase *is* important and should not be omitted. As Dr. Stone pointed out in this regard, "The reasons for the necessity of active rest (Rejuvenation) are not completely clear but certainly it contributes to the reduction of physical and mental (especially emotional) fatigue. Thus it reduces the possibility of overtraining during the next cycle."

In order for the concept of periodization to be fully understood, we urge you now to examine the following chart outlining the way it works.

One thing you must remember about periodization is this: as the body adapts, you have to continue to stress it. And, as your level of strength grows, you have to load yourself more heavily to keep making gains. Even though the Hypertrophy phase calls for "light" weights, the target weight (See

Periodization

Period	Phase	Description	Duration	Sets and Repetitions
One	Hypertrophy	High volume (High repetitions) Low intensity (Light weights)	4 weeks	1 set of 10 with warm-up weight 1 set of 10 with intermediate weight 3 sets of 10 with target weight
Two	Basic Strength	Moderate volume (Moderate repetitions) Medium intensity (medium weights)	4 weeks	1 set of 10 with warm-up weight 1 set of 5 with intermediate weight 3 sets of 5 with target weight 1 set of 10 with 70% of target weight*
Three	Power	Low volume (Low repetitions) High intensity (Heavy weights)	2 weeks	1 set of 10 with warm-up weight 1 set of 3 with light intermediate weight 1 set of 3 with intermediate weight 3 sets of 3 at target weight 1 set of 10 with 70% of target weight*
Four	Rejuvenation (Active Rest)	Very low volume (Few repetitions; light forms of other exercise) Very low intensity (Very light weights or no weight training)	1 to 2 weeks	Do no organized weight work. Experiment with new exercises: cycle, play racquetball, swim, etc. Do not try to keep making gains.

*These single sets with 70%—sometimes called "down sets"—help to maintain the gains in lean body weight made during Hypertrophy.

page 28 for information on how to choose your target weight) would only be light for you if you had to lift it but once or twice. Even in hypertrophy, your target weight should be heavy for you to use for 3 sets of 10 repetitions.

We recommend further, at least for the first couple of cycles, that 3 sets of repetitions, rather than 5, be done in each exercise in which you are using the target weight for the day. For instance, if you were in the Hypertrophy stage of your training, this would mean that you would want to do 3 sets of 10 repetitions with your goal weight for the day. If that goal weight was 135 pounds, say, you'd do a *warm-up* of 10 reps with around 95 pounds, an intermediate set of 10 reps with 115 pounds, and then you'd jump to 135 pounds for 3 sets of 10 before going on to your next exercise. So, your full workout would consist of 5 sets of 10, even though only 3 of those sets would be at your "target weight" for the day.

As for the exercises, we outline our particular recommendations in the following sections of the book. What exercises you choose will depend on the equipment available to you. Any weight-training exercise can be used in a periodization program. The only weight-training exercises that are different are abdominal exercises such as sit-ups and leg raises. We say this *not* because the muscles involved wouldn't adapt well to periodization but because it is technically difficult to attach enough weight to the legs, for instance, so that 2 or 3 reps in the leg raise would be your limit. So, just do higher reps in your waist work and work as quickly as you can.

The main thing you'll need to do with periodization is to choose weights that are close to your limit for your sets at the "target weight." What we mean by "target weight" is that if your routine calls for 3 sets of 10 repetitions in the squat, you should be able to make all 10 reps in all 3 sets with the same poundage. The tenth rep in the third set should be a tough one—even the last 3 or 4 repetitions should be. *But don't miss.* Forgive us for harping on this, but periodization is based on the body's *gradual accommodation* to the increasingly heavy loads with which you exercise. Make sure you allow your body time to adjust. Be conservative about your increases from week to week to insure that you can make all the reps for the right number of sets. *This is especially important during your first, basic training cycle,* when you will be primarily adjusting yourself to your new exercise program.

If you haven't trained with weights at all before, it might be a good idea for you to think of your first twelve-week cycle as part of a larger "macrocycle." Perhaps if you can visualize it as the foundation cycle for two or three other cycles that you will also do in the coming year, it will allow you to accept the fact that you need to be realistic and conservative in your approach to the first cycle and that you especially need to choose weights you can handle for all the desired repetitions. With one cycle under your lifting belt, you'll know your body better, and you can then afford to be a bit more adventurous and push yourself a bit harder. Just remember, you've got a lot of good, productive years ahead of you—don't rush things.

Naturally, on your first cycle, you'll need to spend some time working into the program. Remember, it took three full weeks for the members of the sedentary women's study to work in to the full routine. If you have not been involved in any sort of exercise program, please make sure to do as the women in our study did and adjust yourself gradually to the increased activity. You'll still feel some soreness and stiffness at first—what Selye calls the alarm stage—but don't take a week off because of it, or you'll have to go through the pain again. Just follow our suggestions, don't neglect your stretching and don't do more than we suggest, even though you may feel as if you can.

In the research work done on periodization, and this is crucial, it was found that the greatest strength increases occurred when a particular group of muscles was stressed really vigorously—maximally—only once a week. In our recommendations we have followed this principle, designating one day a "heavy day" and one a "light day" in the basic program, in which you train only twice a week. As you train longer, you may wish to train more days per week, but even in more complicated routines, it is still important that you vary the resistance from day to day and that a "light" and a "heavy" day be designated for each body part per week. This allows the body adequate rest, and you'll progress much faster than if you try to go heavy at each workout. The light day, however, is not a cakewalk. It is designed to be approximately 85 percent as heavy as your other training day, which, if you're doing as you should and choosing weights that really tax you on your heavy day, will still make this light day vigorous. For example, if you did 3 sets of 10 with 100 pounds on Thursday in the squat, on your light day the following Sunday, you'd use 85 pounds as your target weight for 3 sets of 10.

The final thing we need to discuss is choosing your target weights. In this, working with someone who's done some weight training is really valuable to a beginner, because what seems hard to a beginner is often not hard when viewed in light of the enormous capabilities of the human body. Even so, during the Hypertrophy stage, your target weights for the first couple of weeks should seem relatively easy. You shouldn't feel exhausted or be sopping with sweat when you finish. Remember, you are using very light weights, at first, to prevent soreness. At the end of Hypertrophy, however, you should be using a weight for your 3 sets of 10 that *will* make you perspire, that *will* make your heart pump vigorously, and that you can barely lift for the final few reps of that third set. Understandably, there's no way for us to predict what that weight will be for you. Men and women have very different natural levels of strength, as do people of different ages and activity levels. The best advice we can give is for you to choose a target weight for your heavy day that you can use for all 3 sets of 10, a weight that is, on the final set, quite hard for you to lift the required number of times. After you've gone through a couple of cycles, you'll understand a lot more about your body's limitations and will be able to judge your poundages pretty accurately.

Sometimes, despite your best intentions, you'll miss some of your repetitions on a particular day. If this happens, *do not increase the weights on your next heavy day,* but repeat the workout of the previous week and try hard to get the desired number of repetitions. Never move up in weight until you have done your 3 full sets with the right weight for the scheduled number of reps.

Naturally, sometimes you'll make an increase that is beyond you, but when this happens, simply repeat the same weight—unless the weight was obviously *far* too heavy—the next week on your heavy day. In the beginning it is better to use weights that are too light rather than too heavy. A good rule of thumb is to make the smallest possible increases from week to week, unless those small increases don't properly tax the muscles. One way you can tinker with this program to make each workout more tailored to your strength level on any given day is to move your target weight up, or even down, 5 or 10 pounds after your *first* target-weight set. By doing this, you can adjust the resistance so that it is appropriate to your strength level. This should make your second and third target-weight sets what they should be—tough but achievable.

Two other questions that should be answered here are how long to rest between sets and how much weight to use on warm-up and intermediate sets. The answer to the first question is that you should train as fast as you *comfortably* can. Obviously, you shouldn't do 10 reps with your target weight and immediately do 10 more. As a matter of fact, you shouldn't be *able* to do this since it would imply that you were using too light a target weight. A good guideline is to take your next set as soon as you feel able to lift the weight the designated number of repetitions. As soon as your breathing begins to return to normal, take the next set. You'll soon learn how long you need to rest. The key is to rest as little as possible and still use substantial weight.

The answer to the question of what weights to use on your warm-up and in intermediate sets can vary, but good ball-park figures are 65 to 70 percent of your target weight on your warm-up set and 80 to 85 percent on your intermediate set. If you've stretched properly, you'll already be fairly well warmed up, so 65 to 70 percent should be a safe warm-up weight. Finally, if you're really pushed for time and you feel well warmed after your first set, you *can* skip your intermediate set. We don't recommend this, however, as it lessens your overall workload and consumption of calories.

To give you a little more understanding of how to choose poundages, we made a chart of a full ten-week cycle for a man who's never trained with weights before. Joe Average is forty-five, weighs around 150 pounds and has done no regular exercise for the past ten years.

Joe Average's Training Log

Age: 45   Body weight: 150
(Note: Log entries follow the Weights-Repetitions-Sets format.
125 × 10 = 125 pounds for 1 set of 10 repetitions.
125 × 10 × 3 = 125 pounds for 3 sets of 10 repetitions.)

Hypertrophy

Week One

Monday—Heavy

Flexibility:	Did all 11 stretches twice; held each for 10 count both times
Squats:	Did 2 sets of free squats, 1 set with 45-pound bar
Bench Press:	45 × 10 × 3
Rows:	45 × 10 × 3
Sit-ups:	10 reps

Thursday—Light

Flexibility:	Repeated 11 stretches twice; held for count of 10, then count of 20
Squats:	No weight × 10 (warm-up)
	45 × 10 × 3
Bench Press:	45 × 10 × 4
Rows:	45 × 10 × 4
Sit-ups:	12 reps, 10 reps

Week Two
Monday—Heavy
> *Flexibility:* Repeated 11 stretches twice; held for count of 10, then count of 20
> *Squats:* No weight × 10 (warm-up)
> 45 × 10 (intermediate)
> 60 × 10 × 3 (target)
> *Bench Press:* 45 × 10; 55 × 10; 60 × 10 × 3
> *Rows:* 45 × 10; 55 × 10; 60 × 10 × 3
> *Sit-ups:* 15, 10, 8

Thursday—Light
> *Flexibility:* 11 stretches × 15 count; then 20 count
> *Squats:* No weight × 10; 45 × 10; 50 × 10 × 3
> *Bench Press:* 45 × 10; 50 × 10 × 4
> *Rows:* 45 × 10; 50 × 10 × 4
> *Sit-ups:* 15, 10, 10

Week Three
Monday—Heavy
> *Flexibility:* 11 stretches × 20 count; then 25 count
> *Squats:* 55 × 10; 65 × 10; 75 × 10 × 3
> *Bench Press:* 50 × 10; 60 × 10; 70 × 10 × 3
> *Rows:* 55 × 10; 65 × 10; 70 × 10 × 3
> *Sit-ups:* 18, 12, 10
> *Leg Raises:* 10, 8

Thursday—Light
> *Flexibility:* 11 stretches × 20 count; then 25 count
> *Squats:* 45 × 10; 55 × 10; 65 × 10 × 3
> *Bench Press:* 45 × 10; 55 × 10; 60 × 10 × 3
> *Rows:* 50 × 10; 55 × 10; 60 × 10 × 3
> *Sit-ups:* 20, 15, 12
> *Leg Raises:* 10, 10

Week Four
Monday—Heavy
> *Flexibility:* 11 stretches × 25 count; then 30 count
> *Squats:* 60 × 10; 75 × 10; 95 × 10 × 3
> *Bench Press:* 55 × 10; 70 × 10; 80 × 10 × 3
> *Rows:* 60 × 10; 70 × 10; 80 × 10 × 3
> *Sit-ups:* 22, 18, 15
> *Leg Raises:* 12, 10

Thursday—Light
> *Flexibility:* 11 stretches × 30 count; twice
> *Squats:* 60 × 10; 70 × 10; 80 × 10 × 3
> *Bench Press:* 55 × 10; 65 × 10; 70 × 10 × 3
> *Rows:* 60 × 10; 65 × 10; 70 × 10 × 3
> *Sit-ups:* 25, 20, 20
> *Leg Raises:* 15, 15, 10

Basic strength

Week Five
Monday—Heavy

Flexibility:	11 stretches × 30 count; 11 × 30 count
Squats:	65 × 10; 95 × 5; 115 × 5 × 3; 90 × 10
Bench Press:	60 × 10; 80 × 5; 90 × 5 × 3; 65 × 10
Rows:	65 × 10; 85 × 5; 95 × 5 × 3; 70 × 10
Sit-ups:	25, 25, 25
Leg Raises:	15, 18, 12
Twists:	25, 25

Thursday—Light

Flexibility:	11 stretches × 30 count × 2 sets
Squats:	65 × 10; 90 × 5; 100 × 5 × 3; 80 × 10
Bench Press:	60 × 10; 70 × 5; 75 × 5 × 3; 55 × 10
Rows:	65 × 10; 75 × 5; 80 × 5 × 3; 60 × 10
Sit-ups:	25 × 3
Leg Raises:	20, 15, 15
Twists:	35, 25

Week Six
Monday—Heavy

Flexibility:	11 stretches × 30 count × 2 sets
Squats:	75 × 10; 110 × 5; 125 × 5 × 3; 95 × 10
Bench Press:	65 × 10; 85 × 5; 100 × 5 × 3; 70 × 10
Rows:	75 × 10; 95 × 5; 105 × 5 × 3; 75 × 10
Sit-ups:	25 × 3
Leg Raises:	20 × 3
Twists:	35, 30

Thursday—Light

Flexibility:	11 stretches × 30 count × 2 sets
Squats:	75 × 10; 95 × 5; 105 × 5 × 3; 80 × 10
Bench Press:	65 × 10; 75 × 5; 85 × 5 × 3; 60 × 10
Rows:	70 × 10; 80 × 5; 90 × 5 × 3; 65 × 10
Sit-ups:	25 × 3
Leg Raises:	25 × 2, 20
Twists:	50, 35

Week Seven
Monday—Heavy

Flexibility:	11 stretches × 30 count × 2 sets
Squats:	95 × 10; 125 × 5; 135 × 5 × 3; 95 × 10
Bench Press:	70 × 10; 90 × 5; 105 × 5 × 3; 75 × 10
Rows:	80 × 10; 100 × 5; 110 × 5 × 3; 80 × 10
Sit-ups:	25 × 3
Leg Raises:	25 × 3
Twists:	50 × 2

Thursday—Light

Flexibility:	11 stretches × 30 count × 2 sets
Squats:	90 × 10; 105 × 5; 115 × 5 × 3; 80 × 10
Bench Press:	70 × 10; 80 × 5; 90 × 5 × 3; 65 × 10
Rows:	75 × 10; 85 × 5; 95 × 5 × 3; 70 × 10
Sit-ups:	25 × 3
Leg Raises:	25 × 3
Twists:	50 × 2

Week Eight

Monday—Heavy

Flexibility:	11 stretches × 30 count × 2 sets
Squats:	95 × 10; 130 × 5; 145 × 5 × 3; 100 × 10
Bench Press:	75 × 10; 95 × 5; 110 × 5 × 3; 80 × 10
Rows:	80 × 10; 105 × 5; 115 × 5 × 3; 85 × 10
Sit-ups:	25 × 3
Leg Raises:	25 × 3
Twists:	50 × 2

Thursday—Light

Flexibility:	11 stretches × 30 count × 2 sets
Squats:	90 × 10; 115 × 5; 125 × 5 × 3; 90 × 10
Bench Press:	70 × 10; 85 × 5; 95 × 5 × 3; 70 × 10
Rows:	80 × 10; 90 × 5; 105 × 5 × 3; 70 × 10
Sit-ups:	25 × 3
Leg Raises:	25 × 3
Twists:	50 × 2

Power

Week Nine

Monday—Heavy

Flexibility:	11 stretches × 30 count × 2 sets
Squats:	100 × 10; 130 × 3; 145 × 1; 160 × 3 × 3; 115 × 10
Bench Press:	80 × 10; 90 × 3; 105 × 1; 115 × 3 × 3; 80 × 10
Rows:	90 × 10; 110 × 3; 120 × 3 × 3; 85 × 10
Sit-ups:	25 × 3
Leg Raises:	25 × 3
Twists:	50 × 2

Thursday—Light

Flexibility:	11 stretches × 30 count × 2 sets
Squats:	95 × 10; 115 × 3; 135 × 3 × 3; 95 × 10
Bench Press:	70 × 10; 90 × 3; 100 × 3 × 3; 70 × 10
Rows:	75 × 10; 95 × 3; 105 × 3 × 3; 75 × 10
Sit-ups:	25 × 3
Leg Raises:	25 × 3
Twists:	50 × 2

Week Ten

Monday—Heavy

Flexibility:	11 stretches × 30 count × 2 sets
Squats:	100 × 10; 140 × 3; 155 × 1; 170 × 3 × 3; 120 × 8
Bench Press:	85 × 10; 100 × 3; 110 × 1; 120 × 3 × 3; 85 × 10
Rows:	90 × 10; 115 × 3; 125 × 3 × 3; 90 × 10
Sit-ups:	25 × 3
Leg Raises:	25 × 3
Twists:	50 × 2

Thursday—Light

Flexibility:	11 stretches × 30 count × 2 sets
Squats:	100 × 10; 130 × 5; 145 × 3 × 3; 100 × 8
Bench Press:	75 × 10; 95 × 3; 105 × 3 × 3; 75 × 10
Rows:	80 × 10; 100 × 3; 110 × 3 × 3; 80 × 10
Sit-ups:	25 × 3
Leg Raises:	25 × 3
Twists:	50 × 2

Weeks Eleven and Twelve Rejuvenation

Please remember that the sort of fitness you can achieve through periodization has very little to do with strength for the sake of strength. Your aim is to increase your level of fitness in every way—flexibility, muscular endurance, cardiovascular condition, psychological health, *as well as strength.* Periodization can help you with all of these areas and at the same time not be so terminally boring that you find it hard to decide whether to go to the gym or clean out the septic tank. Overcoming the mental routineness of any sort of training program is tough, but going to the gym and doing the same exercises for the same number of repetitions week after week after week is deadening. And if you're bored, you'll find yourself stopping to talk to your fellow trainers—when you should be pushing ahead, trying to keep your pulse elevated—or skipping certain exercises that you particularly dislike or, what's worse, avoiding the trip to the gym altogether.

The important things to remember with periodization are:

1. Choose weights that are heavy enough to "stress" the muscles without being so heavy you miss any repetitions.
2. Never increase to a heavier weight unless you were able to do all 3 sets of 10 with the target weight for the day the previous week.
3. Make sure to keep your light days "light" by using around 85 percent of the poundage you used on your heavy day.
4. Be patient. Even if you feel really strong, resist the urge to "max out" unless it's the very last workout of the cycle. Then, if you like, do some singles to see what your limits are. Otherwise, train progressively so that your body has time to adapt muscularly and psychologically to the heavier poundages.
5. Be sure to Rejuvenate before you start your next cycle. This is critical.
6. When you start your second cycle, start Hypertrophy at a higher level than you did the cycle before. You don't have to move that first target weight up much from where you started the previous cycle, just enough that you continue to stress the muscles properly.

7. Always remember to do a "down set" of 10 repetitions during the Basic Strength and Power phases of training to maintain your hypertrophy.

8. And, finally, while you are scheduled to do only 3 sets with your target weight, don't forget that you are supposed to also do a warm-up set and an intermediate set before you hit the target. For safety's sake don't neglect these. Even if you're working with a light weight such as 55 pounds, do 45, 50, and then 3 sets at 55. Remember that the *total* workload is important. (Todd & Todd)

CHAPTER 3

Strength Training Principles and Programs

MOTOR UNITS

The human body has about 434 muscle groups that are used to move the various parts of the anatomy. Each one of these muscles is made up of what are known as *motor units.* A motor unit is composed of a single motor neuron and all of the muscle cells innervated by this neuron.

All motor units do not have the same capabilities and are classified as either slow-twitch, fast-twitch a, or fast-twitch b motor units. Table 3.1 summarizes the characteristics of the various motor units. An individual muscle is composed of both fast-twitch and slow-twitch muscle units. Fast-twitch units have the ability to contract very rapidly and thus generate a large amount of force in a short period of time. They expend their energy sources quickly and thus are more easily fatigued.

Slow-twitch units can exert force for longer periods of time and are used for activities that require submaximum force, such as jogging, walking, and long-distance swimming. Even though genetics determines whether we have muscles composed of a greater percentage of slow-twitch units or fast-twitch units, strength training can affect the ability of both units to exert force.

During the contraction of a muscle, motor unit recruitment is greatly affected by the force necessary to perform the movement. Slow-twitch motor units are usually recruited to lift a light weight. However, in lifting a heavy weight, all of the motor units might have to be recruited. *Ramp effect* refers to the relationship between the percentage of muscle fibers used and the amount of muscular force required to recruit motor units. Figure 3.1 illustrates this idea.

One important implication of the ramp effect is how it may affect a strength training program. To increase the potential of all of the motor traits, especially the potential of the fast-twitch motor units, the training must be of a fairly high intensity. The use of a proper strength program allows all of the motor units to be stimulated and thus increases their capability to become stronger and exert a greater force.

Motor unit type is usually determined in the laboratory by an invasive procedure that involves collecting a small sample of muscle tissue using a needle biopsy. The muscle sample is then chemically analyzed to determine the ratio of various motor units contained in the muscle.

Table 3.1	Characteristics of Fast-Twitch (FT$_a$, FT$_b$) and Slow-Twitch (ST) Motor Units		
Characteristic	**ST**	**FT$_a$**	**FT$_b$**
NEURAL ASPECTS			
Motoneuron size	Small	Large	Large
Motoneuron recruitment threshold	Low	High	High
Motor nerve conduction velocity	Slow	Fast	Fast
STRUCTURAL ASPECTS			
Muscle fiber diameter	Small	Large	Large
Mitochondrial density (aerobic energy)	High	High	Low
Capillary density	High	Medium	Low
Myoglobin (aerobic) density	High	Medium	Low
ENERGY SUBSTRATE			
Creatine phosphate stores	Low	High	High
Glycogen (carbohydrate) stores	Low	High	High
Triglyceride (fat) stores	High	Medium	Low
ENZYMATIC ASPECTS			
Glycolytic (anaerobic) enzyme activity	Low	High	High
Oxidative (aerobic) enzyme activity	High	High	Low
FUNCTIONAL ASPECTS			
Twitch (contraction) time	Slow	Fast	Fast
Relaxation time	Slow	Fast	Fast
Force production	Low	High	High
Fatigue resistance	High	Low	Low
DISTRIBUTION			
Endurance athletes	High	Medium to high	Low
Sprint, explosive athletes	Medium to low	Medium to high	High

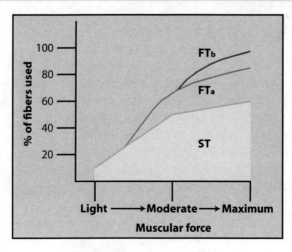

Figure 3.1   Ramp Effect

JOINT-LEVER SYSTEM

Many times when people think of a strength training program, they only consider changes that take place in the muscle tissue. Movement in the body is produced through the use of joint-lever systems, which are composed of nervous tissue, connective tissue, skeletal tissue, and muscle tissue. A proper strength training program may increase the output of a joint-lever system by bringing about changes in one or more of the various tissues. Figure 3.2 is an example of a joint-lever system.

The exact physiological cause of increased strength is not known, but an examination of research reveals that changes that take place in the joint-lever system might contribute to an increase in strength. An indication of these sites is contained in Figure 3.3.

Nervous Tissue

As a result of a strength program, a neural adaptation could bring about an increased neural drive to muscle. This has been indicated by the use of electromyographic (EMG) studies. Other changes in the nervous system may bring about a possible increased synchronization of the motor units that make up the various muscle groups, and this might contribute to increased strength.

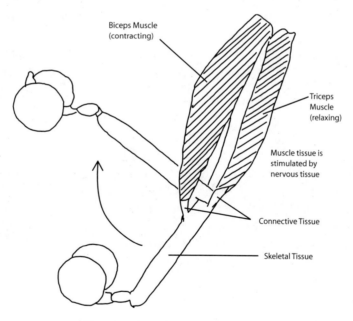

Figure 3.2   Joint-Lever System

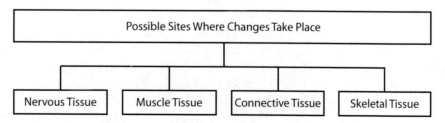

Figure 3.3   Changes in the Joint-Lever System

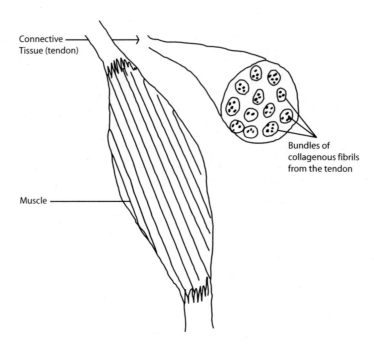

Figure 3.4   Connective Tissue

Sensory units located in the tendons, known as Golgi tendon organs, when stimulated by tension placed on a joint-lever system, cause a muscle to relax. A strength program may bring about changes that partly inhibit this mechanism and allow a greater force to be produced by the muscle. Much of the increased strength output in the first few weeks of a strength training program is thought to be due to changes in the nervous system.

Connective Tissue

The body uses connective tissue to hold bones and muscles together. Connective tissue is also used to transmit the force of a muscle contraction to the bone or lever arm of the joint-lever system. Very few muscles are directly attached to the bone by muscle alone. The muscle is usually attached to a tendon, which is composed of connective tissue. To transmit the force, the connective tissue relies on many collagenous fibrils, which are primarily composed of protein. Figure 3.4 is a diagram of connective tissue. A proper strength training program increases these fibrils and thus increases the capability of connective tissue to transmit force to the bone.

Skeletal Tissue

Skeletal tissue is used to construct the levers in a joint-lever system. A proper strength training program increases the deposit of mineral salts in the skeletal tissue and thus increases bone density.

Osteoporosis is a condition of increased porosity and decreased bone mineral density. More women die each year from problems resulting from hip fractures related to osteoporosis than from the combination of deaths from breast cancer, uterine cancer, and ovarian cancer. Osteoporosis might be prevented if the prevention starts early enough in a person's life. Two major factors that can help to prevent osteoporosis are weight-bearing exercises and a proper diet with adequate calcium. Adolescent boys and girls should have a daily intake of at least 1,200 milligrams of calcium, and adults should take in at least 1,000 milligrams per day. After menopause, women should have a daily intake of at least 1,500 milligrams per day.

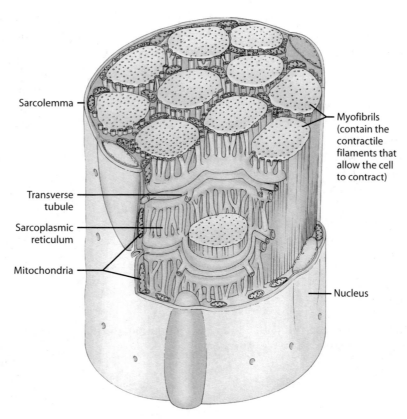

Sarcolemma

Myofibrils
(contain the
contractile
filaments that
allow the cell
to contract)

Transverse
tubule

Sarcoplasmic
reticulum

Mitochondria

Nucleus

Figure 3.5   Muscle Cell

Regular weight-bearing exercise will help prevent osteoporosis. Increasing the amount of resistance, such as in strength training, may provide the body with an effective stimulus to cause an increase in the density of the bone. Research reveals that the forces produced on certain bones, such as the lumbar vertebrae in the back, during walking and jogging are 1.75 times the body's weight. During a strength training program using weights, the loads may be as much as 5 to 6 times the body's weight. Thus, the results of a strength training program have beneficial effects on skeletal tissue.

Muscle Tissue

Because of its ability to contract, muscle tissue is the only tissue in the body that has the capability to produce a force. Figure 3.5 contains a diagram of the components of a muscle cell.

A muscle is made up of many muscle cells known as motor units. To increase the strength of the muscle, usually an increase in the size of the muscle must occur. *Hypertrophy, hyperplasia,* and *atrophy* are terms that are useful in understanding how a muscle might become larger or smaller:

Hypertrophy: Increase in cell size
Hyperplasia: Increase in number of cells
Atrophy: Decrease in cell size and/or a decrease in cell number

Research indicates that the major change in muscle tissue as a result of a strength training program is due to hypertrophy of the muscle cells.

An examination of figure 3.5 reveals that a muscle cell is made up of bundles called myofibrils. Myofibrils contain the contractile filaments that allow the muscle cell to contract. The stimulus of a strength training program appears to release chemical modulators that cause the myofibrils to split and activate chemical mechanisms that increase the amount of contractile filaments within the myofibrils. This increased mass allows the cell to exert a greater force and become stronger.

Muscles can also become weaker through the process of atrophy, which is a decrease in the size of a cell due to loss of myofibrils and contractile filaments. Atrophy also refers to a loss of muscle cells. As explained earlier, a muscle is composed of motor units that are classified as slow-twitch, fast-twitch a, and fast-twitch b motor units. To stimulate or overload the fast-twitch motor units, you must utilize relatively high resistance. If these motor units are not used, they begin to atrophy. The fast-twitch motor units are highly susceptible to atrophy, especially after the age of twenty-five. Once these cells are lost, the body cannot restore them. This is one of the reasons why strength training should be a lifelong activity.

WEAKEST JOINT ANGLE PRINCIPLE

As a joint-lever system goes through a full range of motion, the ability to exert force at different joint angles changes. Figure 3.6 illustrates this concept.

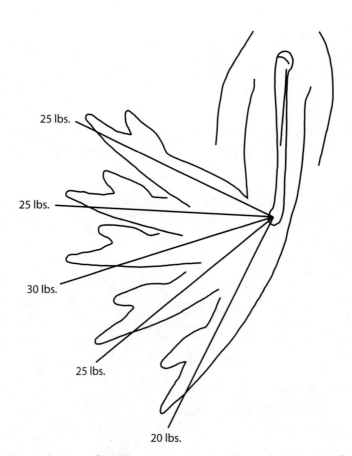

Figure 3.6   Change of Ability to Exert Force Through a Range of Motion

A muscle exerts the greatest force when it is in a slightly stretched position. Another factor that affects the production of force is the mechanical alignment of the bones that make up the lever arms. This factor is referred to as *mechanical advantage,* or the ratio of the force arm to the resistance arm. For example, the most advantageous joint angle during arm flexion, using the biceps, is thought to be approximately when the elbow is flexed at a 100° angle. Thus when a joint-lever system is working through a range of motion, the variables of muscle length and mechanical advantage are going to have an effect on the force produced by the system.

Some machines supposedly have the capability to apply maximum resistance at every joint angle through a range of motion. This might appear to be an advantage, as shown in Figure 3.7. These machines are known as *accommodating resistance machines* and are based on the principle of using either isokinetic or variable resistance. In real-life movements, however, using the joint-lever systems of the body through a full range of motion, the system will always be limited by the weakest joint angle.

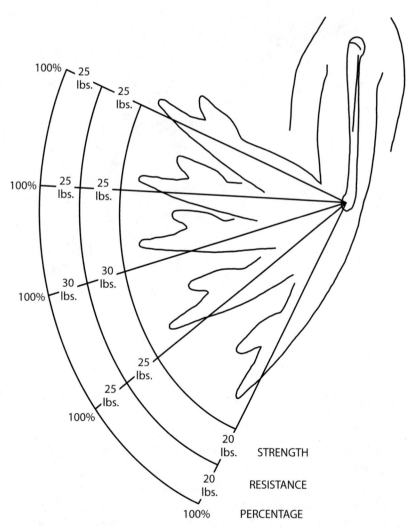

Figure 3.7   Accommodating Resistance Concept

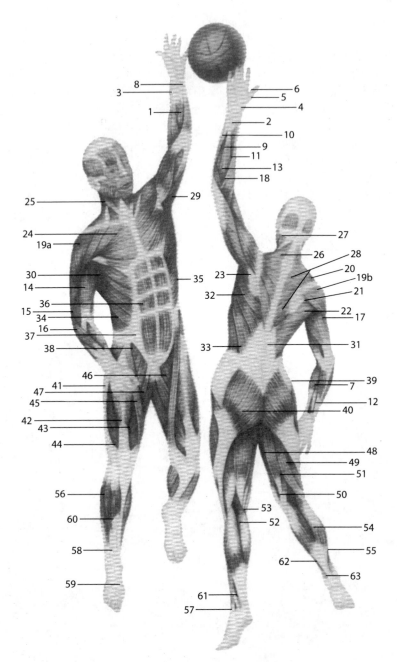

Figure 3.8 Major Human Muscles

MAJOR HUMAN MUSCLES

Familiarity with basic anatomy and various movements of the human body is necessary in designing weight training programs. Figure 3.8 contains a diagram of the major human muscles, and Table 3.2 lists the name of the muscle, the action of the muscle, and the sport in which the muscle is used. By using this information, you can analyze a sport to determine the most important movements and the muscles involved. For example, muscle no. 26, the trapezius, tilts the head back, elevates the shoulder point, and adducts the scapula. This muscle is used in the wrestler's bridge, passing a football, and cleaning a barbell, as well as in the breaststroke, archery, and batting.

Table 3.2	Muscle Action and Sport Use

Supinate: rotate forearm to palms-up
Invert: turn sole of foot inward
Evert: turn sole of foot outward
Elevate: raise a part against gravity
Depress: lower a part, yielding to gravity
Lateral: located toward the outer side
Medial: located toward the middle
Flex: bend at a joint, decreasing angle

Extend: straighten at a joint
Adduct: move toward midline of body
Abduct: move away from midline
Rotate: move part around an axis
Prone: face downward
Supine: face upward
Pronate: rotate forearm to palms-down

Muscle	**Primary Action** (numbers in parentheses indicate muscles that assist)	**Sport in Which Greatest Resistance Is Encountered**
1. Flexor digitorum-profundus	Flexes fingers	Any sport in which one grasps an opponent, partner, or equipment, such as wrestling, hand-to-hand balancing, tennis, horizontal bar, ball bat, etc.
2. Extensor digitorum	Extends fingers	
3. Flexor pollicis longus	Flexes thumb	
4. Extensor pollicis longus	Extends thumb	
5. Abductor pollicis longus	Abducts thumb	
6. Adductor pollicis longus	Adducts and flexes thumb	
7. Flexor carpi radialis	Flexes wrist palmward (8), abducts hand (9)	Tennis, throwing a baseball, passing a football, handball, ring work, two-handed pass in basketball, batting, golf swing
8. Flexor carpi ulnaris	Flexes wrist palmward (7), adducts hand (10)	
9. Extensor carpi radialis longus and brevis	Extends wrist (10), abducts hand (7)	Backhand stroke in tennis and badminton, Olympic weight lifting, bait and fly casting
10. Extensor carpi ulnaris	Extends wrist (9), adducts hand (8)	
11. Pronator teres	Pronates forearm	Tennis forehand, shot put, throwing a punch, throwing a baseball, passing a football
12. Pronator quadratus		
13. Supinator	Supinates forearm (16)	Throwing a curve ball, batting, fencing thrust
14. Biceps brachii	Flexes forearm (16)	Ring work, rope climb, archery, pole vaulting, wrestling, backstroke in swimming
15. Brachialis		
16. Brachioradialis	Flexes forearm, supinates forearm	Rowing, cleaning a barbell, rope climb
17. Triceps brachii	Extends forearm	Breaststroke, shot put, parallel bar work, vaulting, hand shivers in football, hand balancing, batting pole vaulting, fencing thrust, passing, boxing
18. Anconeus		
19. Deltoid	Abducts humerus (20)	Hand balancing, canoeing, shot put, pole vaulting, tennis, archery, batting, fencing thrust, passing a football, tackling, breaststroke, back and crawl strokes, golf swing, handball
Anterior fibers	Flexes humerus	
Posterior fibers	Extends humerus	
20. Supraspinatus	Abducts humerus (19)	
21. Infraspinatus	Rotates humerus laterally	
22. Teres minor		

Continued.

Table 3.2   Muscle Action and Sport Use—Cont'd

Muscle	Primary Action (numbers in parentheses indicate muscles that assist)	Sport in Which Greatest Resistance Is Encountered
23. Teres major	Adducts, extends, and rotates humerus medially (32)	Rope climb, canoe racing, ring work, rowing, batting, crawl, back, breast, and butterfly strokes, pole vaulting, golf
24. Pectoralis major	Adducts, flexes, and rotates humerus	Tackling, crawl, and backstrokes, tennis, passing a football, throwing a baseball, javelin, pole vaulting, wrestling, shot put, discus throw, straight-arm lever position in gymnastics, punching
25. Sternocleidomastoid	Flexes and laterally flexes neck, rotates head (27)	Crawl stroke, tucking chin in wrestling, football, boxing, distance running (breathing)
26. Trapezius	Bends head laterally toward shoulder Elevates shoulder Adducts scapula	Wrestler's bridge Passing a football, cleaning a barbell, breaststroke Archery, batting, breaststroke
27. Splenius cervicis/capitus	Extends head back Extends head (26) Rotates head	
28. Major and minor rhomboids, levator scapulae	Adducts and rotates scapula medially, depresses shoulder	Tennis backhand, batting, back and breaststroke
29. Subscapularis	Rotates humerus medially (24), stabilizes humerus in glenoid cavity to prevent displacement	Tackling, crawl and backstrokes, tennis, passing a football, throwing a baseball, javelin, pole vaulting, wrestling, shot put, discus throw, straight-arm level position in gymnastics
30. Serratus anterior	Abducts scapula	Shot put, discus throw, tennis, archery, tackling, crawl stroke, passing a basketball, passing a football, punching
31. Erector spinae	Extends vertebral column	Discus and hammer throw, batting, golf swing, racing start in swimming, diving and tumbling, rowing, blocking in football
32. Latissimus dorsi	Adducts, extends, and rotates humerus medially; depresses shoulder	Rope climb, canoe racing, ring work, rowing, batting, crawl, back, breast, and butterfly strokes, pole vaulting, golf swing

Continued.

Table 3.2	Muscle Action and Sport Use—Cont'd	
Muscle	**Primary Action** (numbers in parentheses indicate muscles that assist)	**Sport in Which Greatest Resistance Is Encountered**
33. Quadratus lumborum	Flexes vertebral column, flexes vertebral column laterally	The importance of this group in all sports, posture, and general fitness and appearance cannot be overstated
34. External abdominal oblique 35. Internal abdominal oblique 36. Rectus abdominus 37. Transverse abdominus	Flexes and rotates vertebral column Flexes vertebral column (33) Compresses abdomen	The importance of this group in all sports, posture, and general fitness and appearance cannot be overstated
38. Iliopsoas, pectineus	Flexes femur (42)	Running, hurdling, pole vaulting, kicking a football, line play, flutter kick, pike and tuck positions in diving and tumbling
39. Gluteus medius	Abducts femur, rotates femur medially	Hurdling, fencing, frog kick, shot put, running, line play, skating
40. Gluteus maximus 41. Tensor fasciae	Extends femur, rotates femur laterally Flexes, abducts, and rotates femur medially	Skiing, shot put, running, quick starts in track, all jumping and skipping, line play, skating, swimming start, changing directions while running
42. Rectus femoris 43. Vastus medialis 44. Vastus lateralis 45. Sartorius	Extends lower leg (43, 44), flexes femur Extends lower leg Flexes lower leg, flexes femur, rotates femur laterally	Skiing, skating, quick starts, all jumping, kick in football or soccer, flutter kick, frog kick, water skiing, diving, trampoline and tumbling, bicycling, catching in baseball
46. Adductor magnus 47. Adductor longus 48. Gracilis	Adducts femur (48) Adducts femur, flexes lower leg	Skiing, skating, frog kick, broken field running, bareback horseback riding
49. Biceps femoris 50. Semimembranosus 51. Semitendinosus 52. Popliteus	Flexes lower leg, rotates lower leg laterally (53, 54); extends femur (48, 50, 51) Flexes lower leg, rotates lower leg medially (52) Extends femur Flexes lower leg, rotates lower leg medially	Skiing, skating, quick starts in track and swimming, hurdling line play, all jumping
53. Plantaris 54. Gastrocnemius 55. Soleus 56. Peroneus longus 57. Peroneus brevis	Plantar flexes foot (when knee is almost straight) Flexes lower leg Plantar flexes foot Plantar flexes and everts foot	Quick starts in track, swimming, basketball, football, skating, all jumping, skiing Changing directions while running, skating, skiing, running, all jumping, racing starts, skating turns

Continued.

Table 3.2	Muscle Action and Sport Use—Cont'd	
Muscle	**Primary Action (numbers in parentheses indicate muscles that assist)**	**Sport in Which Greatest Resistance Is Encountered**
58. Extensor digitorum	Extends the four smaller toes	
59. Extensor hallicus	Extends the big toe	
60. Tibialis anterior	Dorsiflexes and inverts foot	
61. Tibialis posterior	Plantar flexes and inverts foot	
62. Flexor digitorum longus	Flexes the four smaller toes	
63. Flexor hallicus longus	Flexes the big toe	

Source: Adapted from Muscle Action Chart by Cramer Products, Inc. Reprinted by permission of Cramer Products, Inc., P.O. Box 1001, Gardner, KS 66030.

Regardless of the training method chosen, the overload principle, discussed next, must be utilized to obtain strength gains, and the resistance must be progressively increased as the muscles increase in strength.

OVERLOAD PRINCIPLE

In any physical fitness program, the *overload principle* refers to the requirements necessary to bring about improvement in the various systems of the body. As the body is subject to loads greater than those to which the systems are accustomed, the various systems adjust and increase their capacity to perform physical work.

A classic example concerns the Greek hero Milo of Crotona. Each day Milo lifted a calf to his shoulders and ran through the stables. As the calf grew and added body weight, the increased weight provided the overload necessary to bring about the physiological changes in Milo's body systems to make him stronger. The same principle accounts for increased strength in any training program.

One contemporary example demonstrating the overload principle is the jogger who first runs only one mile and then each week adds another mile to the training program. Because of this overload, certain systems of the body are stimulated and increase their ability to perform the work of jogging. In time the jogger will easily be able to cover ten or more miles on a training run.

Specific body systems require specific overloads. In jogging, for instance, the cardiovascular system requires an overload that is different from the overload necessary to bring about strength gains. This is referred to as the *law of specificity*. The minimum resistance that a person can use and still be confident of obtaining strength gains is approximately 60 percent of the maximum force that a muscle group can exert. The following chapters contain all of the information necessary to ensure that the specific overload for strength will be contained in the planning of a strength training program.

BASIC DEFINITIONS

Before organizing a strength program, familiarity with the following definitions is necessary:

> *Accommodating resistance:* the use of a machine that adjusts the resistance in an attempt to obtain maximum resistance through a full range of motion
> *Barbell:* a bar with iron plates attached

> *Bodybuilder:* a person who uses weight training to obtain a more muscular physique; a physique athlete
>
> *Concentric action:* a shortening of the muscle against resistance
>
> *Dumbbell:* a hand weight
>
> *Dynamic action:* muscle action with movement
>
> *Eccentric action:* a lengthening of the muscle against resistance
>
> *Free weights:* barbells and dumbbells; free weights differ from strength training machines, which are restricted on how they can be used
>
> *Isokinetic training:* the use of a machine that controls the speed of a muscle contraction and attempts to vary the resistance according to the muscle force applied
>
> *Isometric action:* muscle action without movement
>
> *Maximum resistance:* maximum weight lifted in one repetition of an exercise
>
> *Muscular endurance:* the ability to perform repeated muscle movements for a given period of time
>
> *Periodization:* dividing the training year into periods and manipulating the stress of training to combat overtraining
>
> *Physique:* the body structure; organization or development of the physical appearance
>
> *Progressive resistance training:* increasing the amount of weight lifted as one becomes stronger
>
> *Recovery period:* the rest interval time between sets
>
> *Repetition maximum:* the maximum amount of weight lifted for a given number of repetitions. For example, 1 RM would be the maximum weight lifted for one repetition, and 6 RM would be the maximum weight lifted for six repetitions
>
> *Repetitions:* the number of times an exercise is performed
>
> *Set:* a given number of repetitions
>
> *Strength:* the ability to exert force against resistance
>
> *Variable resistance training:* the use of a machine that adjusts the resistance through the range of movement of a muscle contraction to accommodate to the change in muscle strength at different joint angles
>
> *Weight lifting:* competition that requires the participants to use specific lifts
>
> *Weight training:* a systematic series of resistance exercises to develop strength

STRENGTH PROGRAMS

Strength development programs are basically either *dynamic* (muscle actions with movement) or *isometric* (muscle actions with little or no movement).

The most common type of training program is one using dynamic actions. The major advantage of this system is that it brings about strength gains through a full range of motion. As a muscle goes through a range of motion, it must receive adequate resistance at all of the joint angles to stimulate strength increases. For example, if resistance is incurred at only the 90° angle, this is where the muscle will be stronger, not at the other angles, where resistance is not encountered. Dynamic training seems to have a greater effect on muscle hypertrophy, muscle endurance, increased flexibility, and development of connective tissue. This type of training also allows the individual to observe the work being done, which can be a source of satisfaction from a psychological standpoint.

From a cosmetic viewpoint, the gains made from a dynamic program are greater than those from an isometric program. Since many people engage in strength programs for body changes related to training, this is an added benefit for dynamic training.

Some advantages ascribed to an isometric training program are that it requires less equipment and usually causes little muscle soreness. This mode of training makes it possible to isolate specific joint angles to strengthen. In one program, specific isometric actions with the leg muscles were used to increase the ability of various athletes to jump higher and farther. The primary training program, however, for the athletes was dynamic; isometric exercises were utilized to supplement this program.

A disadvantage of isometric training is that it may causes high systolic and diastolic blood pressures, which might be harmful to the heart and circulatory system.

MACHINES VS. FREE WEIGHTS

In the past few years, as interest in the development of strength has increased, a dazzling array of exercise machines has appeared on the market. Advertisements use highly persuasive language to explain why their specific machines are best and why all other machines and training methods will soon be obsolete. Many advertisements contain testimonies from prominent athletes or coaches.

With the development of these machines have come new terms in strength training: *isokinetic* and *variable resistance.* As a muscle goes through a range of motion, the ability of the lever system to exert force changes at different angles. Thus the amount of weight that can be lifted is limited by the weakest point in the range of motion. Therefore many manufacturers of equipment have developed machines that theoretically have the ability to adjust the resistance of the machine to the muscle's ability to exert force. The claim is that these machines will bring about a faster and greater increase of strength through the full range of motion.

The other type of training devices are sometimes referred to as *free weights.* Free weights include barbells, dumbbells, and other related equipment. In the early 1900s, Allan Calvert developed adjustable barbells, with which weighted plates could be added or taken off to change the resistance. In over one hundred years, few changes have been made to alter his basic design.

Many discussions have taken place regarding the merits of machines versus free weights. Some observers believe that it is not an either-or problem; rather, a trainer should use many different methods in strength training. As long as the basic principles regarding strength development are observed, making strength gains and body changes with both machines and free weights is possible. Being consistent in your training in the program you choose is probably more important than the type of training device you select. The best recommendation is to experiment with different exercises and various types of training equipment and use them to develop a personalized program. (Allsen)

CHAPTER 4

Weight Management = Nutrition + Activity

Good, sound nutritional choices are necessary for maintaining a healthy lifestyle. Making the effort to obtain the essential nutrients through daily dietary intake is not something in which most Americans are proficient. In general, Americans eat too much salt, sugar, and fat and do not consume the recommended daily allowance (RDA) of vitamins and minerals.

Poor dietary habits, along with being physically inactive, is one of the major factors that results in Americans becoming increasingly overweight and obese. As noted in chapter 3, being overweight or obese is a major risk factor for chronic health problems such as hypertension, cardiovascular disease, diabetes, and certain types of cancers. With this in mind, the importance of building a knowledge base that will allow an individual to develop sound, lifelong nutritional habits and practices becomes clear.

Once an individual has made the effort to gather information that will allow him or her to make good nutritional choices, he or she must then make a concentrated effort to obtain the essential macronutrients and micronutrients through their daily food selections. **Macronutrients** provide energy in the form of calories. Carbohydrates, fats, and proteins make up the sources of macronutrients. Micronutrients, which include vitamins and minerals, regulate bodily functions such as metabolism, growth, and cellular development. Together, macronutrients and micronutrients are responsible for the following three tasks that are necessary for the continuance of life:

1. growth, repair, and maintenance of all tissues,
2. regulation of body processes, and
3. providing energy.

Because nutrition information if often filled with scientific terminology and unfamiliar jargon, it is many times misleading or appears to be overly complicated. Several government agencies, such as the United States Department of Agriculture and the Department of Health and Human Services, have teamed up in an effort to simplify and streamline nutritional information widely available to the general public in an effort to decrease the amount of misinformation on nutrition and increase the prevalence of practical, easily to apply, user-friendly information.

Table 4.1	Good Sources of Dietary Fiber

Fruits	Grams
1 medium apple	4–5
1 banana	3
1 cup blueberries	5
10 dates	7
1 orange	3
1 pear	5
1 cup strawberries	3
1 watermelon slice	2–3

Vegetables	Grams
1 artichoke	4
1 raw carrot	2
½ cup cream style corn	6
1 cup chopped lettuce	1
½ cup green peas	6
1 cup cooked spinach	6
1 cup cooked squash	5–6
1 tomato	2

Legumes	Grams
1 cup cooked black beans	15
1 cup cooked green beans	3
1 cup pork and beans	18
1 cup cooked blackeyed peas	11
1 cup kidney beans	20
1 cup cooked navy beans	16
1 cup cooked pinto beans	19

Grains	Grams
1 bagel	1
1 whole grain slice of bread	1–3
4 graham crackers	3
1 bran muffin	2
hot dog/hamburger bun	1
1 cup cooked oatmeal	7–9
½ cup Grape Nuts cereal	3.5
1 cup Nature Valley granola	7.5
¾ cup Shredded Wheat cereal	4
1 cup cooked macaroni	1
1 cup cooked rice	2.5–4
1 cup cooked spaghetti	1–2

Other	Grams
1 cup almonds	15
1 cup cashews	8
1 cup shredded coconut	11
1 tbsp peanut butter	1
¼ cup sunflower seeds	2

ESSENTIAL NUTRIENTS

It is necessary for an individual to ingest more than forty different nutrients in order to maintain good health. Because no single food source contains all of these nutrients, variety in one's diet is essential. Eating a wide variety of foods will help ensure adequate intake of carbohydrates, fats, proteins, vitamins, and minerals.

CARBOHYDRATES

Carbohydrates should be the body's main source of fuel. Between 55 and 60 percent of an individual's diet should be composed of carbohydrates. Of this 55 to 60 percent, 45 to 50 percent of total daily

Table 4.2	What is Your Limit on Fat for the Calories You Consume?		
Total Calories per Day	**Saturated Fat in Grams**		**Total Fat in Grams**
1,600	18 or less		53
2,000*	20 or less		65
2,200	24 or less		73
2,500*	25 or less		80
2,800	31 or less		93

*Percent Daily Values on Nutrition Facts Labels are based on a 2,000 calorie diet. Values for 2,000 and 2,500 calories are rounded to the nearest 5 grams to be consistent with the Nutrition Facts Label.

caloric intake should be from complex carbohydrates, leaving simple carbohydrates to account for less than 10 percent of the daily carbohydrate intake.

Complex carbohydrates are relatively low in calories (four calories per gram), nutritionally dense, and are a rich source of vitamins, minerals, and water. Complex carbohydrates provide the body with a steady source of energy for hours. The best sources of complex carbohydrates are breads, cereals, pastas, and grains.

Dietary fiber, also known as roughage or bulk, is a type of complex carbohydrate that is present mainly in leaves, roots, skins, and seeds and is the part of a plant that is not digested in the small intestine. Dietary fiber helps decrease the risk of cardiovascular disease and cancer, and may lower an individual's risk of coronary heart disease.

Dietary fiber is either soluble or insoluble. **Soluble fiber** dissolves in water. It helps the body excrete fats and has been shown to reduce levels of blood cholesterol and blood sugar, as well as helping to control diabetes. Water soluble fiber travels through the digestive tract in gel-like form, pacing the absorption of cholesterol, which helps prevent dramatic shifts in blood sugar levels. Soluble fiber is found primarily in oats, fruits, barley, and legumes.

Insoluble fiber does not dissolve easily in water; therefore, it cannot be digested by the body. Insoluble fiber causes softer, bulkier stool that increases peristalsis. This, in turn, reduces the risk of colon cancer by allowing food residues to pass through the intestinal tract more quickly, limiting the exposure and absorption time of toxic substances within the waste materials. Primary sources of insoluble fiber include wheat, cereals, vegetables, and the skins of fruits.

The recommended daily intake of fiber is 25–30 grams per day. Health disorders associated with low fiber intake include constipation, diverticulitis, hemorrhoids, gall bladder disease, and obesity. Problems associated with ingesting too much fiber include losses of calcium, phosphorous, iron, and disturbances of the gastrointestinal system.

Simple carbohydrates are sugars that have little nutritive value beyond their energy content. Sugars that are found naturally in milk, fruit, honey, and some vegetables are examples of simple carbohydrates. Foods high in simple sugars are sometimes dismissed as "empty calories." Examples of these foods include candy, cakes, jellies, and sodas.

FATS

Fats are the body's primary source of energy, and supply the body with nine calories of energy per gram ingested. While many Americans consume too many of their daily calories from fats (37 to 40 percent), dietary fat is not necessarily a "bad" component of an individual's diet at moderate levels of consumption. At moderate amounts, between 25 and 30 percent of daily calories, fat is crucial to good nutrition.

Fat has many essential functions: providing the body with stored energy, insulating the body to preserve body heat, contributing to cellular structure, and protecting vital organs by absorbing shock. Fat not only adds flavor and texture to foods and helps satisfy an individual's appetite because it is digested more slowly, it also supplies the body with essential fatty acids and transports fat soluble vitamins A, E, D, and K. Fat is also necessary for normal growth and healthy skin, and is essential in the synthesis of certain hormones.

There are different types of dietary fat. **Saturated fats** are found primarily in animal products such as meats, lard, cream, butter, cheese, and whole milk. However, coconut and palm oils are two plant sources of saturated fat. A defining characteristic of saturated fats is that they typically do not melt at room temperature (an exception being the above mentioned oils that are "almost solid" at room temperature). Saturated fats increase low density lipoproteins (LDL) or "bad cholesterol" levels and in turn increase an individuals risk for heart disease and colorectal cancer.

Trans fat is different from other types of fat in that it typically does not occur naturally in plant or animal products. While a small amount of trans fat is found naturally, the majority of trans fat is formed when liquid oils are made into solid fats (i.e., shortening and some margarines). Trans fat is made during hydrogenation—when hydrogen is added to vegetable oil. This process is used to increase the shelf life of foods and to help foods maintain their original flavor. Many fried foods and "store bought" sweets and treats have high amounts of this type of fat. While most individuals consume four to five times more saturated fat than trans fat, it is important to be aware of the amount of trans fat in one's diet because it raises LDL, "bad," cholesterol and increases the risk of coronary heart disease. Starting January 1, 2006, the Food and Drug Administration requires all foods to list the amount of trans fat contained in the product on the Nutrition Facts panel.

Unsaturated fats are derived primarily from plant products such as vegetable oils, avocados, and most nuts, and do not raise the body's blood cholesterol. Unsaturated fats include both monounsaturated and polyunsaturated fats. **Monounsaturated fats** are found in foods such as olives, peanuts, canola oil, peanut oil, and olive oil. **Polyunsaturated fats** are found in margarine, pecans, corn oil, cottonseed oil, sunflower oil, and soybean oil (see Table 4.3).

Fats become counterproductive to good health when they are consumed in excess. Too much fat in many Americans' diets is the reason Americans lead the world in heart disease. Excess fat intake elevates blood cholesterol levels and leads to atherosclerosis, or a hardening of the arteries. Diets with

Table 4.3	Composition of Oils (%)		
Type	**Sat**	**Poly**	**Mono**
safflower	9	75	16
sunflower	10	66	24
corn	13	59	28
soybean	14	58	28
sesame	14	42	44
peanut	17	32	51
palm	49	9	42
olive	14	8	78
canola	7	35	58

Table 4.4   Percentage of Fat Calories in Foods

Type of Food	Less than 15% of Calories from Fat	15%–30% of Calories from Fat	30%–50% of Calories from Fat	More than 50% of Calories from Fat
Fruits and Vegetables	Fruits, plain vegetables, juices, pickles, sauerkraut		French fries, hash browns	Avocados, coconuts, olives
Bread and Cereals	Grains and flours, most breads, most cereals, corn tortillas, pitas, matzoh, bagels, noodles and pasta	Corn bread, flour tortillas, oatmeal, soft rolls and buns, wheat germ	Breakfast bars, biscuits and muffins, granola, pancakes and waffles, donuts, taco shells, pastries, croissants	
Dairy Products	Nonfat milk, dry curd cottage cheese, nonfat cottage cheese, nonfat yogurt	Buttermilk, low-fat yogurt, 1% milk, low-fat cottage cheese	Whole milk, 2% milk, creamed cottage cheese	Butter, cream, sour cream, half & half, most cheese, (including part-skim and lite cheeses)
Meats		Beef round; veal loin, round, and shoulder; pork tenderloin	Beef and veal, lamb, fresh and picnic hams	All ground beef, spareribs, cold cuts, beef, hot dogs, pastrami
Poultry	Egg whites	Chicken and turkey (light meat without skin)	Chicken and turkey (light meat with skin, dark meat without skin), duck and goose (without skin)	Chicken/turkey (dark meat with skin), chicken/turkey bologna and hot dogs, egg yolks, whole eggs
Seafood	Clams, cod, crab, crawfish, flounder, haddock, lobster, perch, sole, scallops, shrimp, tuna (in water)	Bass and sea bass, halibut, mussels, oyster, tuna (fresh)	Anchovies, catfish, salmon, sturgeon, trout, tuna (in oil, drained)	Herring, mackerel, sardines
Beans and Nuts	Dried beans and peas, chestnuts, water chestnuts		Soybeans	Tofu, most nuts and seeds, peanut butter
Fats and Oils	Oil-free and some lite salad dressings			Butter, margarine, all mayonnaise (including reduced-calorie), most salad dressings, all oils
Soups	Bouillons, broths consomme	Most soups	Cream soups, bean soups, "just add water" noodle soups	Cheddar cheese soups, New England clam chowder
Desserts	Angel food cake, gelatin, some new fat-free cakes	Pudding, tapioca	Most cakes, most pies	
Frozen Desserts	Sherbert, low-fat frozen yogurt, sorbet, fruit ices	Ice milk	Frozen yogurt	All ice cream

Source: American Heart Association/USDA.

Choose Sensibly for Good Health

- Choose a diet that is low in saturated fat and cholesterol and moderate in total fat.
- Choose beverages and foods to moderate your intake of sugars.
- Choose and prepare foods with less salt.
- If you drink alcoholic beverages, do so in moderation.

Fats and Oils

- Choose vegetable oils rather than solid fats (meat and dairy fats, shortening).
- If you need fewer calories, decrease the amount of fat you use in cooking and at the table.

Meat, Poultry, Fish, Shellfish, Eggs, Beans, and Nuts

- Choose two to three servings of fish, shellfish, lean poultry, other lean meats, beans, or nuts daily. Trim fat from meat and take skin off poultry. Choose dry beans, peas, or lentils often.
- Limit your intake of high-fat processed meats such as bacon, sausages, salami, bologna, and other cold cuts. Try the lower fat varieties (check the Nutrition Facts Label).
- Limit your intake of liver and other organ meats. Use egg yolks and whole eggs in moderation. Use egg whites and egg substitutes freely when cooking since they contain no cholesterol and little or no fat.

Dairy Products

- Choose fat-free or low-fat milk, fat-free or low-fat yogurt, and low-fat cheese most often. Try switching from whole to fat-free or low-fat milk. This decreases the saturated fat and calories but keeps all other nutrients the same.

Prepared Foods

- Check the Nutrition Facts Label to see how much saturated fat and cholesterol are in a serving of prepared food. Choose foods lower in saturated fat and cholesterol.

Foods at Restaurants or Other Eating Establishments

- Choose fish or lean meats as suggested above. Limit ground meat and fatty processed meats, marbled steaks, and cheese.
- Limit your intake of foods with creamy sauces, and add little or no butter to your food.
- Choose fruits as desserts most often.

Following the tips above will help you keep your intake of saturated fat at less than 10 percent of calories. They will also help you keep your cholesterol intake less than the Daily Value of 300 mg/day listed on the Nutrition Facts Label.

Table 4.5   USDA Food Guide

The suggested amounts of food to consume from the basic food groups, subgroups, and oils to meet recommended nutrient intakes at twelve different calorie levels. Nutrient and energy contributions from each group are calculated according to the nutrient-dense forms of foods in each group (e.g., lean meats and fat-free milk). The table also shows the discretionary calorie allowance that can be accommodated within each calorie level, in addition to the suggested amounts of nutrient-dense forms of foods in each group.

Daily Amount of Food from Each Group (vegetable subgroup amounts are per week)

Calorie Level	1,000	1,200	1,400	1,600	1,800	2,000	2,200	2,400	2,600	2,800	3,000	3,200
Food Group	Food group amounts shown in cup (c) or ounce-equivalents (oz-eq), with number of servings (srv) in parentheses when it differs from the other units. See note for quantity equivalents for foods in each group. Oils are shown in grams (g).											
Fruits	1 c	1 c	1.5 c	1.5 c	1.5c	2 c	2 c	2 c	2 c	2.5 c	2.5 c	2.5 c
	(2 srv)	(2 srv)	(3 srv)	(3 srv)	(3 srv)	(4 srv)	(4 srv)	(4 srv)	(4 srv)	(5 srv)	(5 srv)	(5 srv)
Vegetables	1 c	1.5 c	1.5 c	2 c	2.5 c	2.5 c	3 c	3 c	3.5 c	3.5 c	4 c	4 c
	(2 srv)	(3 srv)	(3 srv)	(4 srv)	(5 srv)	(5 srv)	(6 srv)	(6 srv)	(7 srv)	(7 srv)	(8 srv)	(8 srv)
Dark green veg.	1 c/wk	1.5 c/wk	1.5 c/wk	2 c/wk	3 c/wk	3 c/wk	3 c/wk	3 c/wk	3 c/wk	3 c/wk	3 c/wk	3 c/wk
Orange veg.	.5 c/wk	1 c/wk	1 c/wk	1.5 c/wk	2 c/wk	2 c/wk	2 c/wk	2 c/wk	2.5 c/wk	2.5 c/wk	2.5 c/wk	2.5 c/wk
Legumes	.5 c/wk	1 c/wk	1 c/wk	2.5 c/wk	3 c/wk	3 c/wk	3 c/wk	3 c/wk	3.5 c/wk	3.5 c/wk	3.5 c/wk	3.5 c/wk
Starchy veg.	1.5 c/wk	2.5 c/wk	2.5 c/wk	2.5 c/wk	3 c/wk	3 c/wk	6 c/wk	6 c/wk	7 c/wk	7 c/wk	9 c/wk	9 c/wk
Other veg.	4 c/wk	4.5 c/wk	4.5 c/wk	5.5 c/wk	6.5 c/wk	6.5 c/wk	7 c/wk	7 c/wk	8.5 c/wk	8.5 c/wk	10 c/wk	10 c/wk
Grains	3 oz-eq	4 oz-eq	5 oz-eq	5 oz-eq	6 oz-eq	6 oz-eq	7 oz-eq	8 oz-eq	9 oz-eq	10 oz-eq	10 oz-eq	10 oz-eq
Whole grains	1.5	2	2.5	3	3	3	3.5	4	4.5	5	5	5
Other grains	1.5	2	2.5	2	3	3	3.5	4	4.5	5	5	5
Lean meat and beans	2 oz-eq	3 oz-eq	4 oz-eq	5 oz-eq	5 oz-eq	5.5 oz-eq	6 oz-eq	6.5 oz-eq	6.5 oz-eq	7 oz-eq	7 oz-eq	7 oz-eq
Milk	2 c	2 c	2 c	3 c	3 c	3 c	3 c	3 c	3 c	3 c	3 c	3 c
Oils	15 g	17 g	17 g	22 g	24 g	27 g	29 g	31 g	34 g	36 g	44 g	51 g
Discretionary calorie allowance	165	171	171	132	195	267	290	362	410	426	512	648

USDA Food Guide

excess fat have attributed to 30 to 40 percent of all cancers in men and 60 percent of all cancers in women, and have also been linked to cancer of the breast, colon, and prostate more frequently than any other dietary factor.

By following the tips listed in the box on page 54, the level of saturated fat and trans fat consumed each day can be limited to 10 percent of that day's total calories.

PROTEIN

Even though **proteins** should make up only 12–15 percent of total calories ingested, they are the essential "building blocks" of the body. Proteins are needed for the growth, maintenance, and repair of all body tissues, i.e., muscles, blood, bones, internal organs, skin, hair, and nails. Proteins also help maintain the normal balance of body fluids and are needed to make enzymes, hormones, and antibodies that fight infection.

Proteins are made up of approximately twenty amino acids. An individual's body uses all twenty of these amino acids in the formation of different proteins. Eleven of the twenty are **non-essential amino acids**—they are manufactured in the body if food proteins in a person's diet provide enough nitrogen. Nine of the twenty are **essential amino acids**—the body cannot produce these, and thus must be supplied through an individual's diet. All amino acids must be present at the same time for particular protein synthesis to occur.

The suggested RDA of protein for adults is forty-five through sixty-five grams per day (intake should not exceed 1.6 gr./kg. of body weight (kg. = 2.2 lbs)). A few exceptions to this rule should be noted: overweight individuals need slightly less than the calculated "norm," and women who are pregnant or lactating need slightly more protein per pound of body weight than the calculation indicates.

It is inadvisable to consume more protein than the daily recommended dosage (45–65 gr./day), particularly in the form of protein supplements. Excessive protein supplementation can damage the kidneys, increase calcium excretion, negatively affect bone health, inhibit muscle growth, and can be detrimental to endurance performance.

VITAMINS

Vitamins are necessary for normal body metabolism, growth, and development. They do not provide the body with energy, but they do allow the energy from consumed carbohydrates, fats, and proteins to be released. Although vitamins are vital to life, they are required in minute amounts. Due primarily to adequate food supply, vitamin deficiencies in Americans are rare. However, there are some situations that may alter an individual's requirements, including pregnancy and smoking. Non-smokers need to consume 60 mg of vitamin C each day; a smoker must ingest 100 mg of vitamin C each day in order to gain the same nutritional benefits. A man or a non-pregnant woman should consume 180–200 mg of folic acid, while a pregnant woman should consume approximately 400 mg of folic acid per day.

Vitamins are grouped as either fat-soluble or water-soluble. **Fat-soluble vitamins** are transported by the body's fat cells and by the liver. They include vitamins A, E, D, and K. Fat-soluble vitamins are not excreted in urine; therefore, they are stored in the body for relatively long periods of time (many months), and can build up to potentially toxic levels if excessive doses are consumed over time.

Water-soluble vitamins include the B vitamins and vitamin C. These vitamins are not stored in the body for a significant amount of time, and the amounts that are consumed and not used relatively quickly by the body are excreted through urine and sweat. For this reason, water-soluble vitamins must be replaced daily.

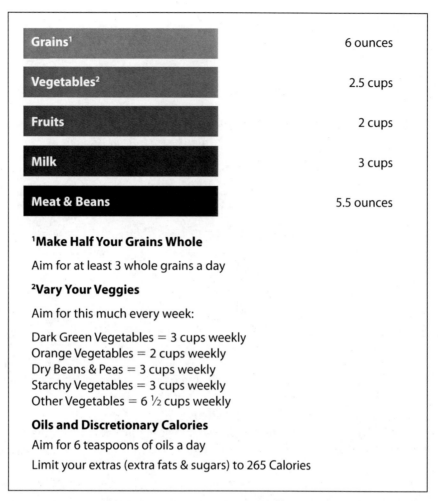

Grains[1]	6 ounces
Vegetables[2]	2.5 cups
Fruits	2 cups
Milk	3 cups
Meat & Beans	5.5 ounces

[1]Make Half Your Grains Whole

Aim for at least 3 whole grains a day

[2]Vary Your Veggies

Aim for this much every week:

Dark Green Vegetables = 3 cups weekly
Orange Vegetables = 2 cups weekly
Dry Beans & Peas = 3 cups weekly
Starchy Vegetables = 3 cups weekly
Other Vegetables = 6 ½ cups weekly

Oils and Discretionary Calories

Aim for 6 teaspoons of oils a day

Limit your extras (extra fats & sugars) to 265 Calories

Figure 4.1   Daily diet recommendations based on a
2000 calorie pattern of a 19 year old female who does less than thirty
minutes of physical activity a day. Go to MyPyramid.gov to get your
personalized diet recommendation.
From www.mypyramid.gov

MINERALS

Minerals are inorganic substances that are critical to many enzyme functions in the body. Approximately twenty-five minerals have important roles in bodily functions. Minerals are contained in all cells and are concentrated in hard parts of the body—nails, teeth, and bones—and are crucial to maintaining water balance and the acid-base balance. Minerals are essential components of respiratory pigments, enzymes, and enzyme systems, while also regulating muscular and nervous tissue excitability, blood clotting, and normal heart rhythm.

Two groups of minerals are necessary in an individual's diet: macrominerals and microminerals. **Macrominerals** are the seven minerals the body needs in relatively large quantities (100 mg or more each day). These seven minerals are: calcium, chloride, magnesium, phosphorus, potassium, sodium, and sulfur. In most cases, these minerals can be acquired by eating a variety of foods each day.

While **microminerals** are essential to healthy living, they are needed in smaller quantities (less than 100 mg per day) than macrominerals. Examples of these minerals include chromium, cobalt, copper, fluoride, iodine, iron, manganese, molybdenum, selenium, and zinc.

Table 4.6	Antioxidants and Their Primary Food Sources
Vitamin A	Fortified milk; egg yolk; cheese; liver; butter; fish oil; dark green, yellow, and orange vegetables and fruits
Vitamin C	Papaya, cantaloupe, melons, citrus fruits, grapefruit, strawberries, raspberries, kiwi, cauliflower, tomatoes, dark green vegetables, green and red peppers, asparagus, broccoli, cabbage, collard greens, orange juice, and tomato juice
Vitamin E	Vegetable oils, nuts and seeds, dried beans, egg yolk, green leafy vegetables, sweet potatoes, wheat germ, 100 percent whole wheat bread, 100 percent whole grain cereal, oatmeal, mayonnaise
Carotenoids	Sweet potatoes, carrots, squash, tomatoes, asparagus, broccoli, spinach, romaine lettuce, mango, cantaloupe, pumpkin, apricots, peaches, papaya
Flavenoids	Purple grapes, wine, apples, berries, peas, beets, onions, garlic, green tea
Selenium	Lean meat, seafood, kidney, liver, dairy products, 100 percent whole grain cereal, 100 percent whole wheat bread

ANTIOXIDANTS

Antioxidants are compounds that aid each cell in the body facing an ongoing barrage of damage resulting from daily oxygen exposure, environmental pollution, chemicals and pesticides, additives in processed foods, stress hormones, and sun radiation. Studies continue to show the ability of antioxidants to suppress cell deterioration and to "slow" the aging process. Realizing the potential power of these substances should encourage Americans to take action by eating at least five servings of a wide variety of fruits and vegetables each day.

There are many proven health benefits of antioxidants. Vitamin C speeds the healing process, helps prevent infection, and prevents scurvy. Vitamin E helps prevent heart disease by stopping the oxidation of low-density lipoprotein (the harmful form of cholesterol); strengthens the immune system; and may play a role in the prevention of Alzheimer's disease, cataracts, and some forms of cancer, providing further proof of the benefits of antioxidants.

Progressive Effects of Dehydration	
Percent loss of body water	**Some progressive effects of dehydration**
0–1 percent	Thirst
2–5 percent	Dry mouth, flushed skin, fatigue, headache, impaired physical performance
6 percent	Increased body temperature, breathing rate, and pulse rate; dizziness, increased weakness
8 percent	Dizziness, increased weakness, labored breathing with exercise
10 percent	Muscle spasms, swollen tongue, delirium
11 percent	Poor blood circulation, failing kidney function

Adapted with permission from "The American Dietetic Association's Complete Food and Nutrition Guide" (Minneapolis: Chronimed Publishing, 1996), p. 168.

WATER

In many cases, **water** is the "forgotten nutrient." Although water does not provide energy to the body in the form of calories, it is a substance that is essential to life. Among other things, water lubricates joints, absorbs shock, regulates body temperature, maintains blood volume, and transports fluids throughout the body, while comprising 60 percent of an individual's body.

While it is clear that adequate hydration is crucial to proper physiological functioning, many people are in a semi-hydrated state most of the time. Whether exercising or not, hydration should be a continuous process. Prolonged periods of dehydration can result in as much as a 10 percent loss of intracellular water concentration and can result in death. Individuals more susceptible to dehydration include: persons who are overweight; deconditioned or unacclimitized to heat; very old and very young; and individuals who do not eat breakfast or drink water.

To ensure proper water balance and prevent dehydration, approximately six to eight eight-ounce glasses of water should be consumed each day an individual is not exercising. When working out, current recommendations for water intake are two to three eight-ounce cups of water before exercising, four to six ounces of cool water every fifteen minutes during the workout, and rehydrating thoroughly after the activity.

THE FOOD GUIDE PYRAMID

The Food Guide Pyramid was originally created in 1992 by the federal government in an attempt to arm more Americans with the knowledge that would allow them to create a healthy, balanced, and tasty diet. Twelve years later, in 2004, the United States Department of Agriculture has produced an expanded and updated version of that original Food Guide Pyramid (see Figure 4.2). Key to the new pyramid is the acknowledged necessity of balancing what an individual eats with the amount of physical activity in which he or she engages.

To make the Pyramid portray the changes deemed necessary by the United States Department of Agriculture (USDA), to promote optimal health, the pyramid was "flipped" onto its side so that all the food group bands run from the top of the pyramid to its base. The different size of each of the bands indicates how much food should be consumed from each food group. The bands are all wider at the base of the pyramid. This symbolizes the importance of eating, when possible, foods without solid fats and added sugar in each of the six bands or groups within the pyramid.

Grains

The color orange represents grains within the pyramid. When examining options of food choices within this group it is important to not only choose a majority on one's daily calories from grains, but also to remember that it is nutritionally prudent to make half of the grains chosen whole grains. Whole grains are defined by the American Association of Cereal Chemists as "food made from the entire grain seed, usually called the kernel, which consists of the bran, germ, and endosperm. If the kernel has been cracked, crushed, or flaked, it must retain nearly the same relative proportions of bran, germ, and endosperm as the original grain." Examples of easy to find whole grains include brown rice, bulgur (cracked wheat), popcorn, whole rye, wild rice, whole oats/oatmeal, whole grain barley, and whole wheat. Selections of whole grain products from this group will help an individual maximize their intake of dietary fiber as well as other nutrients.

GRAINS	VEGETABLES	FRUITS	MILK	MEAT & BEANS

GRAINS Make half your grains whole	VEGETABLES Vary your veggies	FRUITS Focus on fruits	MILK Get your calcium-rich foods	MEAT & BEANS Go lean with protein
Eat at least 3 oz. of whole-grain cereals, breads, crackers, rice, or pasta every day 1 oz. is about 1 slice of bread, about 1 cup of breakfast cereal, or ½ cup of cooked rice, cereal, or pasta	Eat more dark-green veggies like broccoli, spinach, and other dark leafy greens Eat more orange vegetables like carrots and sweetpotatoes Eat more dry beans and peas like pinto beans, kidney beans, and lentils	Eat a variety of fruit Choose fresh, frozen, canned, or dried fruit Go easy on fruit juices	Go low-fat or fat-free when you choose milk, yogurt, and other milk products If you don't or can't consume milk, choose lactose-free products or other calcium sources such as fortified foods and beverages	Choose low-fat or lean meats and poultry Bake it, broil it, or grill it Vary your protein routine — choose more fish, beans, peas, nuts, and seeds

For a 2,000-calorie diet, you need the amounts below from each food group. To find the amounts that are right for you, go to MyPyramid.gov.

Eat 6 oz. every day	Eat 2½ cups every day	Eat 2 cups every day	Get 3 cups every day; for kids aged 2 to 8, it's 2	Eat 5½ oz. every day

Find your balance between food and physical activity
- Be sure to stay within your daily calorie needs.
- Be physically active for at least 30 minutes most days of the week.
- About 60 minutes a day of physical activity may be needed to prevent weight gain.
- For sustaining weight loss, at least 60 to 90 minutes a day of physical activity may be required.
- Children and teenagers should be physically active for 60 minutes every day, or most days.

Know the limits on fats, sugars, and salt (sodium)
- Make most of your fat sources from fish, nuts, and vegetable oils.
- Limit solid fats like butter, stick margarine, shortening, and lard, as well as foods that contain these.
- Check the Nutrition Facts label to keep saturated fats, *trans* fats, and sodium low.
- Choose food and beverages low in added sugars. Added sugars contribute calories with few, if any, nutrients.

MyPyramid.gov
STEPS TO A HEALTHIER YOU

U.S. Department of Agriculture
Center for Nutrition Policy and Promotion
April 2005
CNPP-15

Figure 4.2 My Pyramid
From www.mypyramid.gov

Vegetables

Green is the color within the pyramid that stands for vegetables. Vegetables are an excellent source of natural fiber, they are low in fat, and provide the body with vitamins, especially vitamins A and C. While all vegetables are good nutritional choices, to maximize the benefits of eating vegetables, one should vary the type of vegetables eaten. It is also important when choosing vegetables to ingest not only a variety of the brightly colored vegetables such as corn, squash, and peas, but also the green and orange vegetables such as, carrots, yams, and broccoli. One serving from the vegetable group equals 1 cup of raw, lefty greens; 1/2 cup of other chopped vegetables; or 3/4 cup of vegetable juice.

Fruits

Fruits are represented in the pyramid by the color red. Fresh, canned, frozen, or dried fruits are all excellent sources of vitamins and minerals, most notably vitamin C. It is, however, important to watch for heavy, sugary syrups when selecting canned fruits. Fruits canned in lite syrups or the fruit's own natural juice allow an individual to take in the same amount of vitamins and minerals as their heavily syruped counterparts without adding unnecessary and/or unwanted sugar, fat, and calories to their diet. Fruit juices are another important part of many people's diet that should be monitored for "hidden" sugars and calories. When possible, freshly squeezed juices are an ideal alternative. Serving equivalents for the fruit group are: 1 serving equals 1 medium apple, banana, or orange, 1 melon wedge, 1/2 cup of chopped berries, or 3/4 cup of fruit juice.

Milk

Milk and other calcium-rich foods such as yogurt and cheese now make up the blue portion of the Food Guide Pyramid. Milk products are not only the body's best source of calcium, they are also an excellent source of protein and vitamin B12. To maximize the benefits of calcium-rich foods and minimize the calories, cholesterol, fat, and saturated fat per selection, low-fat and skim alternatives should be chosen. One serving from the milk group equals 1 cup of milk or yogurt, or 1 1/2 oz. of cheese.

Meats and Beans

Purple is the designated color for meats and beans within the pyramid. Meats and beans are excellent sources of protein, iron, zinc, and B vitamins. It is important to be aware of the fact that many food selections within this food group can be relatively high in fat content, especially saturated fats. Lower fat alternatives within this group that remain a rich source of vitamins and minerals include beans, fish, poultry, and lean cuts of beef. Serving equivalents for the meat and beans group are as follows: 1 serving equals 2–3 oz. of cooked lean beef, poultry, or fish; 1 egg; 1/2 cup of cooked beans; or 2 tablespoons of seeds or nuts.

Oils

Oils are depicted by the yellow band within the Food Guide Pyramid. As in all other areas of the pyramid, it is important to choose your source(s) of oils carefully. As a general rule, oils such as olive oil, peanut oil, and canola oil contain unsaturated fats. These oils do not raise an individual's blood cholesterol and are therefore a healthier option.

Daily Activity

The steps along the side of the pyramid symbolize the importance of including exercise into each and every day of a person's life. When daily exercise does not occur, the benefits of even the wisest food or nutrition choices are minimized.

What Happened to the "Fat" Group?

When looking at the new Food Guide Pyramid, it appears that foods like cookies, candies, and sodas found in the former pyramid's "Fat Group" no longer are a part of the pyramid. These foods are typically high in fat, sugars, and "empty" calories, and though they are not mentioned or specifically depicted in the new pyramid, they should only be enjoyed sparingly or in moderation. These foods often taste great but, in general, they provide the body with very little nutritionally.

Due to the fact that one pyramid could not possibly match or meet the needs of all Americans, twelve different Pyramids have been created. To determine which Food Guide Pyramid is the best match, one can go to the United States Department of Agriculture's Web site at MyPyramid.gov and enter their age, gender, and activity level. This process takes only a few seconds and can personalize the amounts and types of grains, vegetables, fruits, milk products, meats, and beans that should be consumed each day to maximize a person's health benefits.

Because an individual's nutritional requirements vary based on their life circumstances, there is a range in the number of servings within each food group. Examples of factors that might influence the number of servings viewed as healthy for an individual could be age, activity level, gender—if the person is a woman, is she pregnant or lactating? The guidelines on the following page are from the U.S. Department of Agriculture, Center for Nutrition Policy and Promotion, and they can help an individual determine the appropriate number of servings from each of the groups within the Food Guide Pyramid based on their current life circumstances.

Determining the appropriate number of servings from each of the food groups is extremely important when planning a healthy diet. However, this information is of little practical value unless a person also knows what constitutes an accurate serving size. Table 4.7 lists serving size equivalents for several common foods.

OTHER ISSUES IN NUTRITION

Vegetarianism

There have always been people who, for one reason or another (religious, ethical, or philosophical), have chosen to follow a vegetarian diet. However, in recent years, a vegetarian diet has become increasingly popular.

There are four different types of vegetarian diets. **Vegans** are considered true vegetarians. Their diets are completely void of meat, chicken, fish, eggs, or milk products. A vegan's primary sources of protein are vegetables, fruits, and grains. Because vitamin B12 is normally found only in meat products, many vegans choose to supplement their diet with this vitamin.

Lactovegetarians eat dairy products, fruits, and vegetables but do not consume any other animal products (meat, poultry, fish, or eggs.)

Ovolactovegetarians are another type of vegetarians. They eat eggs as well as dairy products, fruits, and vegetables, but still do not consume meat, poultry, and or fish.

Table 4.7	How Many Servings Do You Need Each Day?

Food group servings: Perceived, average daily consumed, and recommended* by gender/age group						
	Grains	Fruits	Vegetables	Milk	Meat, etc.	Other (fats, oils, and sweets)
Females 19–24						
Perceived	3.2	2.6	2.6	3.2	3.5	2.2
Consumed	4.2	0.8	1.7	1.2	1.6	3.0
Recommended	9	3	4	2	2.4	Use sparingly
Females 25–50						
Perceived	2.9	2.2	2.5	2.3	3.0	2.1
Consumed	4.6	0.8	2.0	1.0	1.7	3.2
Recommended	9	3	4	2	2.4	Use sparingly
Females 51+						
Perceived	2.5	2.4	2.6	2.1	2.7	1.6
Consumed	4.7	1.5	2.2	1.0	1.7	3.1
Recommended	7.4	2.5	3.5	3	2.2	Use sparingly
Males 19–24						
Perceived	2.9	2.1	2.2	3.1	3.7	2.1
Consumed	5.5	0.6	2.3	1.6	2.3	4.1
Recommended	11	4	5	2	2.8	Use sparingly
Males 25–50						
Perceived	2.9	2.2	2.4	2.2	3.4	2.1
Consumed	5.9	0.9	2.5	1.2	2.5	4.0
Recommended	11	4	5	2	2.8	Use sparingly
Males 51+						
Perceived	2.7	2.2	2.5	2.1	3.1	1.7
Consumed	6.2	1.3	2.7	1.1	2.4	4.5
Recommended	9.1	3.2	4.2	3	2.5	Use sparingly

A person who eats fruits, vegetables, dairy products, eggs, and a small selection of poultry, fish, and other seafood is a partial or **semivegetarian.** These individuals do not consume any beef or pork.

Vegetarians of all four types can meet all their daily dietary needs through the food selections available to them. However, because certain foods or groups of foods that are high in specific nutrients are forbidden, it is critical that a vegetarian is diligent in selecting his or her food combinations so that the nutritional benefits of the foods allowed are maximized. If food combinations from a wide variety of sources are not selected, nutritional deficiencies of proteins, vitamins, and minerals can rapidly occur and proper growth, development, and function may not occur. While a vegetarian diet can certainly be

Table 4.8   Food Guide Pyramid Serving Sizes

The USDA Food Guide Pyramid provides serving size recommendations to guide people in selecting their daily intake.			
	How Many Servings Do You Need Each Day?		
What counts as a serving?	**Children ages 2 to 6, women, some older adults (1600 calories)**	**Older children, teen girls, active women, most men (2200 calories)**	**Teen boys and active men (2800 calories)**
Grains Group (Bread, Cereal Rice, and Pasta)—especially whole grain			
■ 1 slice of bread ■ about 1 cup of ready-to-eat cereal ■ ½ cup of cooked cereal, rice or pasta	6	9	11
Vegetable Group			
■ 1 cup of raw leafy vegetables ■ ½ cup of other vegetables—cooked or raw ■ ¾ cup of vegetable juice	3	4	5
Fruit Group			
■ 1 medium apple, banana, orange, pear ■ ½ cup of chopped, cooked, or canned fruit ■ ¾ cup of fruit juice	2	3	4
Milk, Yogurt and Cheese Group—preferably fat free or law fat			
■ 1 cup of milk** or yogurt ■ 1 ½ ounces of natural cheese (such as Cheddar) ■ 2 ounces of processed cheese (such as American)	2 or 3*	2 or 3*	2 or 3*
Meat and Beans (Meat, Poultry, Fish, Dry Beans, and Nuts)—preferably lean or low fat	2, for a total of 5 ounces	2, for a total of 6 ounces	3, for a total of 7 ounces
■ 2–3 ounces of cooked lean meat, poultry or fish These count as 1 ounce of meat: ■ ½ cup of cooked dry beans or tofu ■ 2½ ounce soyburger ■ 1 egg ■ 2 tablespoons of peanut butter ■ ⅓ cup of nuts			

*Older children and teens ages 9 to 18 years and adults over age 50 need 3 servings daily. Others need 2 servings daily.

**This includes lactose-free and lactose-reduced milk products. Soy-based beverages with added calcium are an option for those who prefer a non-dairy source of calcium.

**University of Michigan
Integrative Medicine**

http://www.med.umich.edu/umim

Healing Foods Pyramid™

University of Michigan Integrative Medicine Clinical Services
© 2004 Regents of the University of Michigan.
Monica Myklebust, MD and Jenna Wunder, MPH, RD
For questions and licensing information please call 734-998-7071

For additional information, or to order your copy, please visit our website at: www.med.umich.edu/umim/clinical/pyramid/.

We emphasize:

- Healing Foods—Only foods known to have healing benefits or essential nutrients are included
- Plant-based choices—Plant foods create the base and may be accented by animal foods
- Variety & balance—Balance and variety of color, nutrients, and portion size celebrate abundance
- Support of a healthful environment—Our food, and we in turn, reflect the health of our earth
- Mindful eating—Truly savor, enjoy and focus on what you are eating

Figure 4.3   Food Guide Pyramid for Vegetarian Meal Planning

With permission of University of Michigan Integrative Medicine http:www.med.umich.edu/umim/clinical/pyramid

a healthy, low-fat alternative to the typical American diet, without diligent monitoring, it is not a guarantee of good health.

For many individuals who choose a vegetarian diet, it is more than simply omitting certain foods or groups of food, it is a way of living that he or she has embraced.

Healthy Food Shopping

The National Heart, Lung, and Blood Institute Obesity Guidelines list the following guidelines to help individuals prepare healthier home cooked meals in shorter periods of time. They suggest reading labels while shopping—paying particular attention to serving sizes and the number of servings within the container. Comparing the total number of calories in similar products and choosing the product containing the lower number of total calories will result in a healthier meal. Finally, make cooking at home easier and healthier by shopping for quick, low fat food items and filling kitchen cabinets with a supply of lower calorie staples such as:

- Fat free or low-fat milk, yogurt, cheese, and cottage cheese
- Light or diet margarine
- Sandwich breads, bagels, pita bread, English muffins, low-fat tortillas
- Plain cereal, dry or cooked
- Rice and pastas, dry beans, and peas
- Fresh, frozen, canned fruits in light syrup or juice
- Fresh, frozen, or no salt added canned vegetables
- Low-fat or no-fat salad dressings and sandwich spreads
- Mustard and ketchup
- Jam, jelly, or honey
- Salsa, herbs, and spices.

Fast Foods/Eating Out

Today, people eat meals outside of their homes more often than ever before. Due to their quick service and comparatively low prices, fast food chains are the most frequent source for meals prepared outside of the home. Each day, millions of people line up inside or drive through outside service lanes of one of the over 140,000 fast food establishments in this country.

When meals are prepared with speed and convenience as the primary focus, good nutrition will, in most cases, suffer. A great majority of fast foods are high in fat, calories, and salt, and low in many of the essential nutrients and dietary fiber.

However, fast food does not have to mean "junk food." While it may take a little more thought and discretion, quick and healthy alternatives do exist. Depending on what ingredients are used and how the food is prepared, fast foods served in restaurants can be healthy. Most restaurants have nutritional information about the foods they serve posted within the dining area or on their menus. By taking a couple of extra minutes to think about their best and most nutritious options, an individual can make dining out more nutritious, filling, and healthy.

Another pitfall of eating meals prepared outside the home is the quantity of food an individual is served. In an effort to be competitive, many restaurants serve well beyond an adequate portion size. To control portion sizes when eating out, order from the senior citizens or kids menus, share the entre with a friend, or take part of the food home for a later meal.

Another way to eat healthy when dining out is to select foods that are steamed, broiled, baked, roasted, or poached rather than foods that are fried or grilled. Asking if the restaurant will trim visible fat off the meat or serve butter, sauces, or dressings "on the side" is yet another way to ensure a healthy and tasty meal.

Dietary Supplements

The best and most preferred method of ingesting an adequate supply of the proper nutrients is to eat a healthy diet consisting of at least five servings of fruits and vegetables. Dietary supplements provide a means to deliver these nutrients to your body in a more convenient, but often less effective, form. For individuals who are considering a dietary supplement, it would be prudent to consult a knowledgeable health professional prior to beginning supplementation. Taken in concentrations higher than the recommended daily allowance, some nutrients have undesirable side effects—some are even toxic.

Many individuals considering dietary supplementation are of the mind set that "if one (or one hundred, etc.) is good, then two will be twice as good!" There is no scientific evidence that this is true. To the contrary, in many cases, excesses of certain nutrients, especially fat-soluble vitamins A, E, D, and K, can become detrimental to the body and can potentially reach toxic levels. Kidney and liver damage, among other health problems, can occur from megadoses of these fat-soluble vitamins and certain minerals. Megadosing on certain vitamins or minerals can also interfere with the absorption of other vital nutrients. For these reasons, consuming more than the recommended daily allowance of vitamins and minerals is discouraged.

There are specific instances in an individual's life when dietary supplementation might be advisable (i.e., pregnancy, anemia and other medical conditions, or certain types of vegetarianism). However, it is recommended that consultation with a registered dietitian or physician occur prior to beginning supplementation, regardless of the situation.

Categories of Weight Loss Products

There are three main categories of weight loss products. Each of these products has the potential to result in the loss of body weight. While some individuals can succeed in losing unwanted pounds through the use of each of these methods, it is important to note both the positive and negative side effects.

Appetite suppressants help diminish a person's appetite, cut cravings, increase their overall level of energy and metabolism, resulting in an increase in the number of calories they burn. While all of the results mentioned will lead to weight loss, it is crucial for an individual to realize that many, if not all, of the products marketed as appetite suppressants can have negative side effects. One major drawback to the use of appetite suppressants is that individuals commonly fail to maintain a well-balanced diet, and this in turn results in deficiencies of important nutrients. Another downside to the use of appetite suppressants that is potentially even more serious is that many times these products contain high levels of caffeine, guarana, or Ma Huang (a herbal form of ephedra) that can cause hypertension, cardiac arrhythmia, myocardial infarction, and/or stroke that can and has led to premature death of the individual consuming this type of dietary supplement. Examples of dietary supplements commonly used include Hydroxycut, Xenadrine-EFX, and Trim Spa. Due to the fact that most, if not all, appetite suppressants do increase an individual's basal metabolism, they can act as metabolism boosters as well as appetite suppressants.

Metabolism boosters are various supplements that speed up or boost an individual's basal metabolism. Most of these types of products act in a way that increases the building of lean muscle mass and decreases the production of fat. Some of these supplements are specific supplements, others are a mixture of several supplements. Metabolism boosters are intended to be used in conjunction with a sound exercise program.

Most of these supplements are all natural. However, most of the products, creatine for example, have not been on the market for a long period of time. Therefore, the long-term effectiveness and safety of these types of supplements are unknown.

Examples of specific supplements include creatine phosphate, chromium picolinate, and HMB. Megathin, Microlean and Metabolife are examples of mixed supplements.

Programs such as Jenny Craig, Weight Watchers, Slimfast and low carbohydrate diets are the final category of weight loss products listed in this text. These products are complete programs for weight loss that suggest a reduced calorie diet. Some programs, such as Jenny Craig and Weight Watchers, have their own prepackaged foods as well as methods of teaching an individual to shop for and consume foods in a particular manner. Other programs, such as Slimfast, replace meals with special "shakes" or "bars."

Of all the programs available currently, a low carbohydrate-high protein diet plan is one of the most popular. The Zone, Atkins Diet, Sugar Busters, Protein Power, and the South Beach Diet are all examples of this type of diet. While there are minor variations within each of the diets, the low

Bar Exam

Energy Bars Flunk

By Bonnie Liebman and David Schardt

"For $50,000 or $100,000 you can be in the bar business," Brian Maxwell, president and CEO of PowerBar Inc, told Food Processing magazine last year.

That's one reason that supermarket, health food store, and drug store shelves carry a burgeoning selection of bars. (You can often find them at the front counter, with the other "impulse" items.) Sales of energy bars rose more than 50 percent last year, to $114 million, according to the trade publication Supermarket News. And energy is just the beginning.

To create a niche for a new bar in a dog-eat-dog marketplace, each manufacturer needs a new twist. Names like Ironman and Steel sell, but they're no longer enough. Viactiv and Luna bars are targeted at women. Protein Revolution, Pure Protein, and Perfect Solid Protein push the nutrient that muscles are made of. GeniSoy and Soy Sensations stake a claim on soy. Clif and Boulder go the natural route. And Think! promises to boost your brain power with herbs and vitamins.

This is one hot market. Why else would Nestlé have bought PowerBar, Kraft have bought Balance Bar, and Rexall Sundown have bought Met-Rx? So when it comes to advertising, chances are we ain't seen nothin' yet.

Do you need any of this stuff? This month we take a look at some of the biggest and boldest bars around. But first, a short course on the "energy" scam.

Energy for Sale

Luckily for food companies out to make a buck, "energy" has a double meaning. To most people, a food that supplies "energy" makes you feel energetic. But to scientists and the literal-minded regulators at the Food and Drug Administration, "energy" means calories.

That's right. To the folks who are in charge of keeping food labels honest, any food with calories is an "energy" food.

Never mind that no more than one in a million consumers would ever guess that, especially when ads for energy bars show people running, leaping, and otherwise looking energetic. Never mind that a simple disclosure on labels could explain to consumers

that an "energy food" means simply that it "contains calories." Years after the Center for Science in the Public Interest (publisher of Nutrition Action) petitioned the FDA to require that kind of disclosure, the agency still hasn't lifted a finger to let consumers in on the energy secret.

Taking advantage of this irresistible loophole, companies have hit on a clever marketing scheme. While few people compete in long-distance athletic events, millions slog through a demanding day with no time for lunch. Marketing "energy" to the average office worker, stay-at-home mom, or just about anyone was a stroke of genius that's paying off big-time. . .but not necessarily for you.

"I caution people not to replace wholesome food with energy bars," says Elizabeth Applegate, a nutritionist and exercise expert at the University of California at Davis. "Manufacturers don't put everything you need from food into them. We don't even know everything in food that *should* be put in them."

Applegate, who consults for the food industry, does advise some people to eat energy bars, but not because they make the eater more energetic. "If you're going to grab a candy bar or a box of cookies or two bags of M&Ms from a vending machine for lunch, it's better to have an energy bar," she says.

Why? 'Most bars are low in saturated and hydrogenated [*trans*] fat. And they can have as much as five grams of fiber and a handful of vitamins and minerals, just like a bowl of breakfast cereal.

"But if the wrappers are starting to accumulate on the floor of your car, back off," she adds. "You're better off with real food, like a sandwich on whole-grain bread, fresh fruit, and some baby carrots."

High-Carb Bars

"Don't bonk," say ads for PowerBars. The original PowerBar, launched in 1987 was designed to keep athletes from bonking—that is, running out of gas in the middle of a marathon or other long-distance event. The high-carbohydrate, low-fat bars consist largely of high-fructose corn syrup and grape and pear juice concentrate, with added vitamins and minerals. They have a taffy-like texture that seems more functional than flavorful.

It didn't take long for competitors (and PowerBar itself) to come up with energy bars that taste more like food than fuel. Clif, Boulder, PowerBar Harvest, and others started adding real food—like oats, nuts, and fruit—to their recipes. The final products taste like something between cookies and granola bars. But judging by the little research that's been done, there's nothing special—other than convenience—about getting your carbs in a compact wrapper.

David Pearson and colleagues at Ball State University in Muncie, Indiana, conducted one of the few studies on high-carb bars, though so far only a summary has been published.[1] First, nine trained cyclists rode for an hour to lower the levels of stored carbohydrate (glycogen) in their muscles. The next day, they rode for another half-hour and then sprinted.

After a one-hour rest, the cyclists were randomly assigned to eat 1,000 calories' worth of PowerBars, Tiger's Milk bars, or cinnamon-raisin bagels over a four-hour period. An hour later, they rode for another hour while the researchers measured their energy output and blood sugar levels.

"The bagels resulted in the same aerobic performance as the energy bars," says Pearson, whose study was funded by Nabisco. "There's no magic to the bars. As long as you're getting the same number of calories and carbs in each food, there's no advantage to eating energy bars, and they're much more expensive."

Of course, most people don't even need carbs when they exercise. "High-calorie, carbohydrate-dense bars are really only for athletes doing long-term exercise," Pearson explains. "People think, 'if top-grade athletes eat these bars, I need them for *my* workout.' That's a misconception."

Pearson's hard-pedaling cyclists performed better with bars (or food) than with just water because they needed carbs. But unless you're running, cycling, cross-country skiing, or doing some other aerobic activity continuously for more than an hour at a stretch, you don't need a quick carb fix.

"The bar wouldn't empty out of your stomach before the event is over," says Pearson. What's more, he adds, "most people burn off fewer calories in the workout than they get from the bar."

So the next time you run a marathon, you may find it easier to pack some high-carb bars instead of bagels. (Some experts recommend taking one bite every ten minutes until the bar is gone.) But if you're just looking for a snack or pick-me-up after a game of tennis, save your money.

40-30-30 Bars

With the high-carb field sewn up, competitors like Balance, Ironman, and ProZone entered the market with bars that have a 40-30-30 ratio of carbohydrates to protein to fat, as touted by the best-selling diet book *The Zone*.

"The companies that market these bars have done a fabulous job of getting people to think that one bar makes their whole diet 40-30-30," notes Applegate.

Reaching 40-30-30 in a bar isn't difficult. It simply means replacing some of the high-fructose corn syrup with protein (from whey or soy protein isolate or casein) and with fat (often palm kernel oil).

Palm kernel oil is popular because it's saturated enough to stay solid at room temperature, so the coating doesn't smear all over your hands. Whether it smears all over the walls of your arteries is another question. Palm kernel oil is twice as saturated as lard.

It's not clear who is supposed to be eating 40-30-30 bars. And that's one secret to their success.

A bar that isn't for anyone in particular is for everyone. They're for athletes (real or would-be) who want to stay "in the zone." (Long before—and one reason why—Barry Sears' diet book became a best seller, that term applied to athletes at the top of their game.) They're for people who want to lose weight. And they're for people who want the "sustained energy" that the bars promise in order to get them through the day.

Of course, no published studies show how 40-30-30 bars like Balance or Ironman affect performance or weight loss for any of those groups. One small study concluded that an Ironman bar didn't raise blood sugar levels as rapidly or as much as a (high-carbohydrate) PowerBar.[2] Of course, a quick rise in blood sugar is precisely what an athlete wants.

"A 40-30-30 bar doesn't have enough carbohydrate for an athlete," says Ball State's Pearson. "But if you're sitting behind a desk and you want a bar instead of a Big Mac for lunch, you're better off with a 40-30-30 bar than a high-carbohydrate bar, because it's closer to what you'd get in a typical American diet."

That's not to say that the highly processed milk and soy protein, high-fructose corn syrup, oils, vitamins, and minerals are anything approaching an ideal food.

Missing are the vegetables, beans, low-fat diary, and other real foods that can cut the risk of cancer, heart disease, and stroke (see cover story).

"If you're using bars in place of a meal, look for at least 10 to 15 grams of protein," says Applegate. "I also recommend eating at least one real food—like a piece of fresh fruit or some carrots or low-fat cheese sticks—with the bar."

Ads boast that the new Balance Gold bars "taste like a candy bar!" That's because they are candy bars. . .with some extra soy or milk protein and vitamins. Balance Outdoor bars use more natural ingredients, like soy pieces, fruit, and nuts. But watch out.

"You can still get a lot of calories from these bars," says Pearson. The 200-odd calories may not seem like much, but 200 calories in roughly two ounces of food means that bars are calorie-dense.

For a quick snack, you're better off with an apple, a handful of grape tomatoes, or some other fruit or vegetable that fills you up with fewer calories.

High-Protein Bars

They've got names like Ultimate Lo Carb, Met-Rx Protein Plus, Promax, Protein Fuel, Protein Revolution, Pure Protein, Solid Protein, and Steel. They're often bigger in calories (250 or so) and size (as much as three ounces), for people who want bigger muscles. Body builders—not dieters, soccer moms, or busy Yuppies—are the typical target audience.

Do They Work?

"Protein needs increase with exercise, whether it's strength training or endurance," says Applegate. But that doesn't mean that people need protein bars.

"You can easily get the protein from food," she explains. "The bars are more expensive and it's just food protein they put in there. People are surprised to hear that. They think, "it's exactly what my muscles need.""

Few companies have studies to show that their "proprietary blends" of milk or soy protein and other ingredients like "growth factors" and glutamine trump the competition.

Take Met-Rx's blend, which is called meta myosyn. Two published studies have tested its impact in healthy people in exercise programs. One found that overweight policemen gained more muscle mass and strength on metamyosyn than they did on another protein supplement, but the measurements were outdated and inexact.[3]

"The results of this study are interesting, but it needs to be repeated using more sophisticated methods of body composition assessment before definitive conclusions can be made," says Rick Kreider of the University of Memphis.

The other study, using more exact measures, found that Met-Rx was no better than a high-carbohydrate supplement at increasing muscle mass and strength in college football players.[4]

Supplement Bars

"Just taste these delicious, satisfying new energy sources for women," say ads for Viactiv. "Boost bars are the ideal snack and help give you the energy to do the things you want to do," says the company's Web site.

Yes, you do get calories from these bars. You also get the same vitamins and minerals that you'd find in a vitamin pill. The main difference is that someone might take a pill along with a bowl of lentil soup, a plate of stir-fried vegetables and chicken, or a fruit salad. But Mead Johnson's clever marketing for its Boost bars persuades people—especially women—to eat a fortified candy bar *instead* of real food. . .and to think they're healthier and more energetic as a result.

Soy protein bars like GeniSoy and Soy Sensations may help lower your cholesterol. But it's too early to say if their phytoestrogens can cut the risk of breast and prostate cancers. In fact, some preliminary studies suggest that consuming more soy may raise the risk of breast cancer in some people (see *Nutrition Action,* Sept. 1999 and Jan./Feb. 2000).

And soy isn't the only new twist. Think! bars sell nothing less than brain power. As if the name weren't enough, the labels and the company Web site (www.thinkproducts.com) note that the bars have "ginkgo biloba to stay sharp" and other "mind enhancing" ingredients, which have an "impact on brain and nerve cell function." But don't expect the company to supply evidence to back up its claims.

"We're not claiming it helps you think," insists Garrett Jennings, the inventor of Think!, the "Food for Thought" bar. Think! bars contain Jennings's secret blend of amino acids, fatty acids, and herbs.

Good published studies show no significant impact on thought or memory in people given the amounts of ginkgo or ginseng (60 mg each) or the other ingredients in Think! Bars. (A recent study found that 160 mg of a proprietary blend of ginseng and ginkgo modestly improved the "quality" of memory in middle-aged men and women, but until it's published, we can't draw any conclusions.)

"But if somebody feels great after a Think! bar," asks Jennings, "who cares if that's just a placebo effect?"

The information for this article was compiled by Jackie Adriano.

[1] *J. Strength Cond. 10:* 1996.

[2] *J. Amer. Diet. Assoc. 100:* 97, 2000.

[3] *Ann. Nutr. Metab. 44:* 21, 2000.

[4] *J. Exercise Physiol.* (online) 2: 24, 1999.

carbohydrate diets basically limit the ingestion of carbohydrate-rich foods such as breads, rice, potatoes, cereal, pasta, juices, sweets, and even fruits and some vegetables. Participants in this type of diet can eat all the protein-rich foods they desire. For example, unlimited portions of steak, ham, bacon, eggs, fish, chicken, and cheese can be consumed.

The basis for this diet is that during digestion, carbohydrates are converted into glucose, which serve as "fuel" for every cell within a person's body. When blood glucose levels begin to rise, insulin, the hormone that allows the entry of glucose into the cells, is released. This process lowers the level of glucose in the bloodstream. If the available glucose is not rapidly used for normal cellular functions or physical activity, the glucose is converted to and stored as body fat. Individual's who support this type of diet believe that if a person eats fewer carbohydrates and more protein, they will produce less insulin, and as insulin levels drop, the body will look to its own fat stores to meet energy needs.

While research has shown that people participating in low carbohydrate-high protein diets do loose weight more rapidly than an individual who maintains a more nutritionally balanced diet but decreases calorie intake and increases physical activity, these same studies show that at the one-year mark weight loss for many of the dieters in both groups was not significantly different. Low carbohydrate diets also have the potential to result in the loss of vitamin B, calcium, and potassium. This can lead to osteoporosis, constipation, bad breath, and fatigue. Because of this and the fact that a diet high in protein, and therefore high in fat, does carry an increased risk for heart disease, it would be prudent for an individual to weigh the benefits of weight loss with the potential negative side effects when looking at this as well as all other types of programs.

Most of these programs include a maintenance plan for individuals to follow once their goal weight has been attained so that the weight lost while participating in the program is not regained.

Fad Diets

Each year billions of dollars are spent in the weight loss industry—unfortunately, many of these dollars are spent on diet plans that are unhealthy, cannot be maintained long term, or simply do not work. The lure of a quick and easy way to "melt away" the pounds is too tempting for many individuals, and although the diets are more times than not ineffective in the long term, weight-loss hopefuls are willing to give almost anything a chance.

To avoid the pitfalls of an unsuccessful, unreliable, or even dangerous weight loss plan, one should always take the time to check out as much factual information as possible from a variety of sources. The boxed information on page 74 is a list of some fad diets that are currently popular and the theories and possible shortcomings within these diets.

Table 4.9   Nutritional Comparison of Energy Bars

High-Carbohydrate Bars (weight of one bar, in ounces)	Calories	Total Fat (grams)	Saturated Fat (grams)	Protein (grams)	Carbohydrates (grams)	Fiber (grams)
✔ ProZone Cashew Almond Crunch (1.8)	190	5	1	7	29	5
✔ Nutra-Fig Cheetah (2.3)[1]	200	2	1	3	44	5
✔ You Are What You Eat (2.0)[1]*	200	4	1	4	40	5
✔ Clif (2.4)[1]*	230	4	1	10	41	5
✔ Boulder (2.5)[1]	210	4	1	10	42	5
✔ PowerBar Harvest (2.3)[1]*	240	4	1	7	45	4
✔ PowerBar Performance (2.3)[1]*	230	2	1	10	45	3
Tiger's Milk (1.2)[1]*	140	4	1	5	22	1
✔ PowerBar Essentials, except Chocolate Raspberry Truffle (1.9)[1]*	180	4	2	10	28	3
PowerBar Essentials Chocolate Raspberry Truffle (1.9)*	180	4	3	10	28	3

Supplement Bars (weight of one bar, in ounces)	Calories	Total Fat (grams)	Saturated Fat (grams)	Protein (grams)	Carbohydrates (grams)	Fiber (grams)
✔ GeniSoy Nature Grains (2.3)[1]	230	3	0	11	41	3
Viactiv Energy Fruit Crispy (1.1)[1]*	120	2	0	4	21	0
✔ TwinLab Soy Sensations, except Chocolate Fondue (1.8)[1]*	180	5	1	15	23	6
✔ Odwalla (2.4)[1]*	240	4	1	7	48	4
✔ Think! Chocolate Mocha (2.0)[1]*	210	4	1	9	36	3
Ensure (1.2)[1]*	130	3	1	6	21	2
Luna (1.7)[1]*	180	4	2	10	25	2
Think!, except Chocolate Mocha (2.0)[1]*	220	7	2	10	33	2
GeniSoy Soy Protein (2.2)[1]*	220	3	2	14	33	1
TwinLab Soy Sensations Chocolate Fondue (1.8)*	180	6	3	15	22	5
Boost (1.6)[1]*	190	6	4	5	30	1
Viactiv Hearty Energy (1.6)[1]*	180	5	4	6	29	0
Think! Divine (1.9)[1]*	210	8	6	6	32	1

High-Protein Bars (weight of one bar, in ounces)	Calories	Total Fat (grams)	Saturated Fat (grams)	Protein (grams)	Carbohydrates (grams)	Fiber (grams)
Met-Rx Natural Krunch (1.1)[1]*	110	2	1	6	18	0
Biochem Ultimate Lo Carb (2.0)[1]*	240	7	1	22	2	0
EAS Myoplex Deluxe (3.2)[1]*	340	7	2	24	44	1
Premier Elite (1.5)[1]	150	3	2	18	2	0

✔ Better Bite = no more than two grams of saturated fat and at least three grams of fiber.
[1]Average of the entire line.
*Fortified with vitamins and minerals.

High-Protein Bars—Cont'd (weight of one bar, in ounces)	Calories	Total Fat (grams)	Saturated Fat (grams)	Protein (grams)	Carbohydrates (grams)	Fiber (grams)
Protein Revolution (2.1)[1]*	230	8	2	22	3	0
PowerBar Protein Plus (2.8)[1]*	290	5	3	24	38	2
EAS Myoplex Lite (2.0)[1]*	190	4	3	15	27	1
SportPharma Extra Protein (2.8)[1]*	280	5	3	31	11	1
TwinLab Protein Fuel (2.9)[1]*	330	5	3	35	12	1
Nature's Best Perfect Solid Protein (2.8)[1]*	270	5	3	32	11	0
Worldwide Sport Nutrition Pure Protein (2.8)[1]*	280	5	3	33	13	0
Biochem Ultimate Protein (2.8)[1]*	290	5	3	31	19	0
American Body Building Hi-Protein Steel Bar (3.0)[1]*	330	6	3	16	52	0
Nature's Best Perfect Isopure (2.1)[1]*	220	6	4	11	36	3
EAS Myoplex HP (2.3)[1]*	250	5	4	20	30	2
Premier Protein (2.5)[1]	290	8	4	31	14	2
MLO BioProtein (2.9)[1]*	300	6	4	21	40	2
Met-Rx SourceOne (2.1)[1]*	170	5	4	16	20	1
SportPharma Promax (2.6)[1]*	280	5	4	20	37	1
EAS Simply Protein (2.8)[1]*	310	7	4	33	16	1
Premier Eight (2.5)[1]	270	6	4	31	7	0
Think! Protein (2.3)[1]*	270	9	5	22	19	0
Met-Rx Protein Plus Food Bar (3.0)[1]*	250	8	6	34	13	0

40/30/30 Bars (weight of one bar, in ounces)	Calories	Total Fat (grams)	Saturated Fat (grams)	Protein (grams)	Carbohydrates (grams)	Fiber (grams)
✔ Balance Outdoor Honey Almond (1.8)	200	6	1	15	21	3
Balance Outdoor Crunchy Peanut (1.8)	200	6	1	15	21	2
Balance Outdoor Nut Berry (1.8)	200	6	1	15	21	2
✔ Balance Outdoor Chocolate Crisp (1.8)	200	6	2	15	21	3
TwinLab Ironman (2.0)[1]*	230	7	2	16	24	0
Balance (1.8)[1]*	200	6	3	14	22	1
Balance + (1.8)[1]*	200	6	4	14	22	1
Balance Gold (1.8)*	210	7	4	15	23	0
ProZone, except Cashew Almond Crunch (1.8)[1]	190	6	5	14	18	5

For Comparison (weight of one bar, in ounces)	Calories	Total Fat (grams)	Saturated Fat (grams)	Protein (grams)	Carbohydrates (grams)	Fiber (grams)
Quaker Chewy Granola (1.0)[1]	120	3	1	2	21	1
Kellogg's Nutri-Grain (1.3)[1]*	140	3	1	2	27	1
Snickers (2.1)	280	14	5	4	35	1
Hershey's Milk Chocolate (1.6)	230	13	9	3	25	1

YOUR BODY AND WEIGHT MANAGEMENT

Body Composition

Body composition is one of the five components of health-related fitness.

An individual's **body composition** measures their percentage of body fat in relation to their percentage of lean body mass (muscle, bone, and internal organs). The ratio of body fat to lean body mass is a better indicator of overall fitness or health rather than a person's actual body weight.

Current thinking suggests an ideal standard of 18 to 23 percent body fat for women and 12 to 18 percent body fat for men. By maintaining a healthy body composition, individuals protect themselves against chronic diseases such as heart disease, stroke, and adult-onset diabetes.

There are several ways to assess body composition that are relatively inexpensive and provide accurate estimates of the percentage of body fat an individual is "carrying." The most common methods for measuring body composition include: hydrostatic or underwater weighing, skinfold thickness, air displacement, and bioelectrical impedance. Because each method gives an estimate of body fat, different methods can yield slightly different results on the same subject. Therefore, it is important when comparing body fat levels (either the same individual's measurement over time or when comparing multiple subjects) that the same method be used at each measurement.

Hydrostatic weighing is one of the most accurate methods of determining the percentage of body fat on an individual. To use this method, the person being weighed sits in a "chair" that is underwater. He or she then exhales the air in their lungs and leans forward keeping their feet on the floor of the tank in which they are submerged. Because the density of lean muscle tissue is different from the density of fat, percentage of body fat can be estimated by the amount of water displaced or by comparing the difference between their underwater weight and their "dry" weight.

While this is an excellent method of determining an individual's body composition, it does have drawbacks. It is difficult to attain accurate results if the person being weighed does not forcefully exhale all of the air in their lungs, does not stay completely underwater the full amount of time necessary to get an accurate measurement (usually about five to ten seconds), or if he or she does not remain calm and still. Also, the procedure should be repeated multiple times for an accurate measurement, making it a relatively time consuming procedure.

Another way body composition can be measured is **skinfold thickness.** This method is based on the notion that half of the body's fat tissue is located directly below the surface of the skin. This technique is performed by a technician that grasps a fold of skin at a specific location and measures it with pressure calipers. For the most accurate results, multiple sites along the individual's right side of their body should be measured. For men, these sites should include the chest, abdomen, and thigh, and for women, the triceps, suprailium, and thigh.

To ensure accuracy, testing should be done at the same time of day, preferably first thing in the morning, because hydration levels can effect the measurement. Also, the same technician should always take a person's measurement because each technician may use a slightly different technique and results could vary slightly with different technicians.

Air displacement is a relatively new method of determining an individual's body composition. With this technique, the person being tested sits inside a small chamber. Pressure sensors determine how much air is displaced by the person inside the chamber and calculate body volume by subtracting the air volume with the person inside the chamber from the air volume of the empty chamber. Body density and percent body fat are then calculated from the body volume obtained.

The main drawback to this technique is that the chamber itself, known commercially as the Bod Pod, is so costly that it is not readily available in fitness centers or even in exercise physiology settings.

Fad Diets

Fad diets are risky because they. . .
- tend to be very low in calories
- are limited to a few foods, limiting key nutrients and minerals
- produce only short-term, rapid weight loss—not long-term weight management
- ignore the importance of physical activity in healthy weight loss
- increase risks for certain diseases or health complications
- take the pleasure and fun out of eating
- alter metabolism, making it easier to regain the weight after the diet has ceased

Diets That Don't Work

1. **"Magical"/Same Foods Diets** (i.e., grapefruit, cabbage soup, Subway diet)
   - *Pros*—usually the single food is a nutritious food
   - *Cons*—too few calories, risk of overeating, lacking of specific nutrients, lack variety, do not teach healthy eating habits, do not encourage exercise
2. **High Protein Diets** (i.e., Atkins)
   - *Pros*—weight loss does occur
   - *Cons*—high in saturated fat and cholesterol increasing risk for heart disease; high protein puts strain on liver and kidneys; lacks vitamins, minerals, complex carbohydrates, and fiber; weight loss is water weight, not fat; lack of carbs causes a condition called ketosis with symptoms of nausea, weakness, and dehydration
3. **Liquid Diets** (i.e., Slimfast)
   - *Pros*—drinks have vitamins, minerals, and high-quality protein
   - *Cons*—do not teach new ways of eating, no long-term weight loss, very low in calories
4. **Gimmicks, Gadgets, and Other "Miracles"**
   - *Pros*—none
   - *Cons*—may be harmful, expensive, do not teach healthy eating, do not encourage exercise

Effective Weight Loss Questionnaire

1. *Could you follow the diet for the rest of your life?* Good health and permanent weight loss require a lifestyle change, not just a temporary modification.
2. *Does the diet promise quick results?* If so, you're probably losing water and lean muscle tissue. Weight loss of ½ lb. to 2 lbs. a week is safe and will more likely be kept off.
3. *Does the diet accommodate your lifestyle?* Any diet that does not allow much freedom or flexibility is less likely to be followed permanently.
4. *Is the diet very low in calories?* Any diet that is below 1,200 calories per day could be dangerous. You may not be getting enough energy and nutrients. You may feel deprived and frustrated, both physically and mentally. In the long run, metabolism slows in order to conserve energy with very low calorie diets.
5. *Does the diet eliminate or restrict certain food groups?* Many diets leave out one or more food groups. Restricting a type of food may result in elimination of essential nutrients in the diet causing health risks. A balanced diet modeled after the Food Guide Pyramid and including a variety of foods should be followed.
6. *Does the diet call for unusual items or require you to go to a specialty store?* Unusual foods or supplements may be very costly and hard to obtain. They may also contain dangerous ingredients that are not regulated by the Food and Drug Administration.
7. *Will someone make money on the diet?* If yes, BEWARE! The diet could be a quick way for someone to make a lot of money.
8. *Is the author or supplier reputable?* To check for validity and credibility of a book, diet, or supplement, view the list of references provided and check the credentials of the author.

One other method of measuring percentage of body fat is **bioelectrical impedance.** The idea behind this technique is that fat tissue is a poorer conductor of electrical current than lean tissue. Therefore, it stands to reason that the easier the conductance, the leaner the individual. Body weight scales with special sensors on the surface can be used to perform this measurement or several sensors can be applied to the surface of the skin that send completely painless electrical currents through the person's body that is being tested (the current estimates body fat, lean body mass, and body water.)

Although this technique is relatively simple and inexpensive to administer, the accuracy of the equations used to estimate body fat are questionable. This technique is nowhere nearly as accurate as hydrostatic weighing, skinfold thickness, or air displacement.

Weight Management

Proper nutrition and regular physical activity are the key components to maintaining or reaching a healthy weight and a healthy body composition. An individual who is overweight is at an increased risk for hypokinetic conditions such as high blood pressure, high cholesterol, stroke, heart disease, obesity, diabetes, and certain types of cancers. For this reason, it is easy to recognize the link between weight management and a long, healthy life.

Because our society has become increasingly automated, Americans are at a greater risk than ever before of developing the hypokinetic conditions associated with being overweight. For most Americans, food is plentiful, and automated equipment and transportation is commonly used to save both time and energy. Therefore, if an individual does not make a concentrated effort to balance physical activity with the calories they consume, poor health or death can occur.

Good, long-term choices in exercise and eating habits are critical. Choosing a healthy assortment of foods based on the recommendations from the Food Guide Pyramid will help in maintaining a healthy weight. Foods that are low in fats and sugars, such as vegetables, fruits, whole grains, skim milk, fish, lean cuts of meat, and beans, are the building blocks of solid nutritional practices.

Another critical component to weight management is choosing sensible portion sizes (see What Counts as a Serving on page 64). Check product labels to learn what quantity of food is considered a serving, and how many calories, grams of fat, etc. are in a serving. Most prepackaged food contains two or more servings—be aware.

What Is a Healthy Body Weight?

The best way to determine overall health in relation to an individual's size is measuring body composition (percentage of body fat in relation to lean body mass). However, there are other easier and/or less costly methods that can give an individual a basic idea of whether or not they fall within a healthy zone based on their body size or weight.

Body Mass Index or BMI, is a quick, easy way to determine whether or not an individual's body weight falls within a healthy range. Although BMI is based on the notion that weight should be proportional to height, it is a more accurate assessment than height-weight charts. The further an individual's BMI is above the healthy range, the higher his or her risk for developing a weight-related condition. Individuals who have a BMI above the healthy range may benefit from weight loss. Table 4.10 shown below contains a Body Mass Index Table and BMI categories.

Ideal Weight versus Natural Weight

Most individuals, particularly females, have an "ideal weight" that they would like to attain. Unfortunately, most of the time this "ideal" is unrealistic. Generally, this perception of perfection is based on

Table 4.10	Body Mass Index Table

To use the table, find the appropriate height in the left-hand column labeled Height. Move across to a given weight *(in pounds)*. The number at the top of the column is the BMI at that height and weight. Pounds have been rounded off.

BMI	19	20	21	22	23	24	25	26	27	28	29	30	31	32	33	34	35
Height (inches)								Body Weight (pounds)									
58	91	96	100	105	110	115	119	124	129	134	138	143	148	153	158	162	167
59	94	99	104	109	114	119	124	128	133	138	143	148	153	158	163	168	173
60	97	102	107	112	118	123	128	133	138	143	148	153	158	163	168	174	179
61	100	106	111	116	122	127	132	137	143	148	153	158	164	169	174	180	185
62	104	109	115	120	126	131	136	142	147	153	158	164	169	175	180	186	191
63	107	113	118	124	130	135	141	146	152	158	163	169	175	180	186	191	197
64	110	116	122	128	134	140	145	151	157	163	169	174	180	186	192	197	204
65	114	120	126	132	138	144	150	156	162	168	174	180	186	192	198	204	210
66	118	124	130	136	142	148	155	161	167	173	179	186	192	198	204	210	216
67	121	127	134	140	146	153	159	166	172	178	185	191	198	204	211	217	223
68	125	131	138	144	151	158	164	171	177	184	190	197	203	210	216	223	230
69	128	135	142	149	155	162	169	176	182	189	196	203	209	216	223	230	236
70	132	139	146	153	160	167	174	181	188	195	202	209	216	222	229	236	243
71	136	143	150	157	165	172	179	186	193	200	208	215	222	229	236	243	250
72	140	147	154	162	169	177	184	191	199	206	213	221	228	235	242	250	258
73	144	151	159	166	174	182	189	197	204	212	219	227	235	242	250	257	265
74	148	155	163	171	179	186	194	202	210	218	225	233	241	249	256	264	272
75	152	160	168	176	184	192	200	208	216	224	232	240	248	256	264	272	279
76	156	164	172	180	189	197	205	213	221	230	238	246	254	263	271	279	287

www.nhlbi.nih.gov

media images, magazine articles, or charts, rather than on reality. The models in advertisements and/or actresses that many women compare themselves to have the luxury of personal trainers, nutrition consultants, and personal chefs, as well as scheduled mandatory exercise sessions. This is not true for the typical woman, therefore, it is unrealistic and can be unhealthy for her to attempt to attain that "look."

When a person eats healthy portions of a variety of foods, their body will reach its natural weight. This is a weight at which the body is comfortable—constant calorie restrictions and hunger are not necessary. Natural weight is a weight which one does not have to struggle in order to maintain.

Determining Caloric Needs

Caloric needs are different for every individual. To a large degree, each person's need is determined by their current body weight and by the level of physical activity they choose to engage in. Outlined in Table 4.11 on page 78 is an easy guide to determining an individual's daily caloric needs.

Department of Health and Human Services • National Institutes of Health

Body mass index (BMI) is measure of body fat based on height and weight that applies to both adult men and women.

BMI Categories:

- Underweight = <18.5
- Normal weight = 18.5–24.9
- Overweight = 25–29.9
- Obesity = BMI of 30 or greater

Figure 4.4   Calculate Your Body Mass Index
Department of Health and Human Services

Guidelines for a Successful Weight Loss Program

The American College of Sports Medicine has put together the following eleven guidelines in an effort to help individuals recognize potentially successful weight loss programs and avoid unsound or dangerous weight loss programs.

1. Prolonged fasting and diet programs that severely restrict caloric intake are scientifically unsound and can be medically dangerous.
2. Fasting and diet programs that severely restrict caloric intake result in the loss of large amounts of water, electrolytes, minerals, glycogen stores, and other fat-free tissues, but with minimal amounts of fat loss.
3. Mild caloric restriction (500–1000 calories less than usual per day) results in smaller loss of water, electrolytes, minerals, and other fat-free tissues and is less likely to result in malnutrition.
4. Dynamic exercise of large muscle groups helps to maintain fat-free tissue, including lean muscle mass and bone density, and can result in a loss of body weight (primarily body fat).
5. A nutritionally sound diet resulting in mild caloric intake restrictions, coupled with an endurance exercise program, along with behavior modification of existing eating habits, is recommended for weight reduction. The rate of weight loss should never exceed 2 lbs. per week.
6. To maintain proper weight control and optimal body fat levels, a lifetime commitment to proper eating habits and regular physical activity is required.
7. A successful weight loss plan can be followed anywhere—at home, work, restaurants, parties, etc.
8. For a plan to be successful, the emphasis must be on portion size.
9. Successful weight loss plans incorporate a wide variety of nutritious foods that are easily accessible in the supermarket.
10. A weight loss plan must not be too costly if it is to be successful.
11. The most essential aspect of a weight loss program is that it can be followed for the rest of an individual's life.

Dieting or cutting back on calories is considered "severe" when an individual ingests fewer than 800 calories in a day. Many physiological problems can result from caloric restrictions of this degree.

Much of the weight lost from "severe" caloric restriction is in the form of muscle. The heart is a muscle, and with severe dieting it can be weakened to the point that it is no longer able to pump blood through the body—resulting in death.

Table 4.11   Estimated Calorie Requirements (in Kilocalories) for Each Gender and Age Group at Three Levels of Physical Activity[a]

Estimated amounts of calories needed to maintain energy balance for various gender and age groups at three different levels of physical activity. The estimates are rounded up to the nearest 200 calories and were determined using the Institute of Medicine equation.

| Gender | Age (years) | Activity Level[b,c,d] | | |
		Sedentary[b]	Moderately Active[c]	Active[d]
Child	2–3	1,000	1,000–1,400[e]	1,000–1,400[e]
Female	4–8	1,200	1,400–1,600	1,400–1,800
	9–13	1,600	1,600–2,000	1,800–2,200
	14–18	1,800	2,000	2,400
	19–30	2,000	2,000–2,200	2,400
	31–50	1,800	2,000	2,200
	51+	1,600	1,800	2,000–2,200
Male	4–8	1,400	1,400–1,600	1,600–2,000
	9–13	1,800	1,800–2,200	2,000–2,600
	14–18	2,200	2,400–2,800	2,800–3,200
	19–30	2,400	2,600–2,800	3,000
	31–50	2,200	2,400–2,600	2,800–3,000
	51+	2,000	2,200–2,400	2,400–2,800

[a]These levels are based on Estimated Energy Requirements (EER) from the Institute of Medicine Dietary References Intakes macronutrients report, 2002, calculated by gender, age, and activity level for reference-sized individuals. "Reference-size," as determined by IOM, is based on median height and weight for ages up to age 18 years of age and median height and weight for that height to give a BMI of 21.5 for adult females and 22.5 for adult males.

[b]Sedentary means a lifestyle that includes only the light physical activity associated with typical day-to-day life

[c]Moderately active means a lifestyle that includes physical activity equivalent to walking about 1.5 to 3 miles per day at 3 to 4 miles per hour, in addition to the light physical activity associated with typical day-to-day life

[d]Active means a lifestyle that includes physical activity equivalent to walking more than 3 miles per day at 3 to 4 miles per hour, in addition to the light physical activity associated with typical day-to-day life.

[e]The calorie ranges shown are to accommodate needs of different ages within the group. For children and adolescents, more calories are needed at older ages. For adults, fewer calories are needed at older ages.

Source: USDA

Severe dieting can also cause an individual's blood pressure to plummet, resulting in dizziness, light-headedness, and fatigue.

EATING DISORDERS

Eating disorders are medically identifiable, potentially life threatening, mental health conditions related to obsessive eating patterns. Eating disorders are not new—descriptions of self-starvation have been found as far back as medieval times.

Top Ten Reasons To Give Up Dieting

10. **DIETS DON'T WORK.** Even if you lose weight, you will probably gain it all back, and you might gain back more than you lost.

9. **DIETS ARE EXPENSIVE.** If you didn't buy special diet products, you could save enough to get new clothes, which would improve your outlook right now.

8. **DIETS ARE BORING.** People on diets talk and think about food and practically nothing else. There's a lot more to life.

7. **DIETS DON'T NECESSARILY IMPROVE YOUR HEALTH.** Like the weight loss, health improvement is temporary. Dieting can actually cause health problems.

6. **DIETS DON'T MAKE YOU BEAUTIFUL.** Very few people will ever look like models. Glamour is a look, not a size. You don't have to be thin to be attractive.

5. **DIETS ARE NOT SEXY.** If you want to be more attractive, take care of your body and your appearance. Feeling healthy makes you look your best.

4. **DIETS CAN TURN INTO EATING DISORDERS.** The obsession to be thin can lead to anorexia, bulimia, bingeing, and compulsive exercising.

3. **DIETS CAN MAKE YOU AFRAID OF FOOD.** Food nourishes and comforts us, and gives us pleasure. Dieting can make food seem like your enemy, and can deprive you of all the positive things about food.

2. **DIETS CAN ROB YOU OF ENERGY.** If you want to lead a full and active life, you need good nutrition, and enough food to meet your body's needs.

And the number one reason to give up dieting:

1. **Learning to love and accept yourself just as you are will give you self-confidence, better health, and a sense of well being that will last a lifetime.**

From Council on Size & Weight Discrimination with permission.

Even though more men are succumbing to eating disorders each year, the mental health condition is typically thought of as a woman's disease. Unfortunately, even grade school girls can feel pressure to "fit in" or look thin. This can be very troubling and disruptive to young girls struggling to build a positive body image.

Typically, a person with an eating disorder seeks perfection and control over their life. Both anorexics and bulimics tend to suffer from low self-esteem and depression. They often have a conflict between a desire for perfection and feelings of personal inadequacy. This person typically has a distorted view of themselves, in that when they look into a mirror, they see themselves differently than others see them. Narcissism, or excessive vanity, can be linked to both anorexia and bulimia.

Eating disorders are often accompanied by other psychiatric disorders, such as depression, substance abuse, or anxiety disorders. Eating disorders are very serious and may be life threatening due to the fact that individuals suffering from these diseases can experience serious heart conditions and/or kidney failure—both of which can result in death. Therefore, it is critically important that eating disorders are recognized as real and treatable diseases.

Anorexia Nervosa

Anorexia Nervosa is a state of starvation and emaciation, usually resulting from severe dieting and excessive exercise. An anorexic will literally stop eating in an effort to control their size.

Most, if not all, anorexic individuals suffer from an extremely distorted body image. People with this disease look in a mirror and see themselves as overweight or fat even when they have become dangerously thin.

Major weight loss is the most visible and the most common symptom of anorexia. Anorexic individuals often develop unusual eating habits, such as avoiding food or meals, picking out a few "acceptable" foods and eating them in small quantities, or carefully weighing and portioning foods. Other common symptoms of this disease include absent menstruation, dry skin, excessive hair on the skin, and thinning of scalp hair. Gastrointestinal problems and orthopedic problems resulting from excessive exercise are also specific to this illness.

Anorexic individuals can lose between 15 and 60 percent of their normal body weight, putting their body and their health in severe jeopardy.

The medical problems associated with anorexia are numerous and serious. Starvation damages bones, organs, muscles, the immune system, the digestive system, and the nervous system.

Between 5 and 20 percent of anorexics die due to suicide or other medical complications. Heart disease is the most common medical cause of death for people with severe anorexia.

Long-term irregular or absent menstruation can cause sterility or bone loss. Severe anorexics also suffer nerve damage and may experience seizures. Anemia and gastrointestinal problems are also common to individuals suffering from this illness.

The most severe complication and the most devastating result of anorexia is death.

Bulimia Nervosa

Bulimia Nervosa is a process of bingeing and purging. This disorder is more common than anorexia nervosa. The purging is an attempt to control body weight, though bulimics seldom starve themselves as anorexics do. They have an intense fear of becoming overweight, and usually have episodes of secretive binge eating, followed by purging, frequent weight variations, and the inability to stop eating voluntarily. Bulimics often feel hunger, overeat, and then purge to rid themselves of the guilt of overeating.

Ways to Love Your Body

■ Become aware of what your body does each day, as the instrument of your life, not just an ornament for others.

■ Think of your body as a tool. Create a list of all the things you can do with this body.

■ Walk with your head held high, supported by pride and confidence in yourself as a person.

■ Do something that will let you enjoy your body. Stretch, dance, walk, sing, take a bubble bath, get a massage.

■ Wear comfortable styles that you really like and feel good in.

■ Decide what you would rather do with the hours you waste every day criticizing your body.

■ Describe 10 positive things about yourself without mentioning your appearance.

■ Say to yourself "Life is too short to waste my time hating my body this way."

■ Don't let your weight or shape keep you from doing things you enjoy.

■ Create a list of people who have contributed to your life, your community, the world. Was their appearance important to their success and accomplishment? If not, why should yours be?

■ If you had only one year to live, how important would your body image and appearance be?

By Margo Maine, Ph.D. and Eating Disorders' Awareness and Prevention

Bulimic individuals are often secretive and discreet and are, therefore, often hard to identify. Typically, they have a preoccupation with food, fluctuating between fantasies of food and guilt due to overeating. Symptoms of bulimia can include cuts and calluses on the finger joints from a person sticking their fingers or hand down their throat to induce vomiting, broken blood vessels around the eyes from the strain of vomiting, and damage to tooth enamel from stomach acid.

Because purging through vomiting, the abuse of laxatives, or some other compensatory behavior typically follows a binge, bulimics usually weigh within the normal range for their weight and height. However, like individuals with anorexia, they often have a distorted body image and fear gaining weight, want to lose weight, and are intensely dissatisfied with their bodies.

While it is commonly thought that the medical problems resulting from bulimia are not as severe as those resulting from anorexia, the complications are numerous and serious. The medical problems associated with bulimia include tooth erosion, cavities, and gum problems due to the acid in vomit. Abdominal bloating is common in bulimic individuals. The purging process can leave a person dehydrated and with very low potassium levels, which can cause weakness and paralysis. Some of the more severe problems a bulimic can suffer are reproductive problems and heart damage, due to the lack of minerals in the body.

Binge-Eating Disorder

People with Binge-Eating Disorder typically experience frequent (at least two days a week) episodes of out of control eating. Binge-Eating episodes are associated with at least three of the following characteristics: eating much more rapidly than normal; eating until an individual is uncomfortably full; eating large quantities of food even when not hungry; eating alone to hide the quantity of food being ingested; feeling disgusted, depressed, or guilty after overeating. Not purging their bodies of the excessive calories they have consumed is the characteristic that separates individuals with Binge-Eating Disorder from those with Bulimia. Therefore, individuals suffering from this disease are typically overweight for their height and weight.

Fear of Obesity

Fear of Obesity is an over-concern with thinness. It is less severe than anorexia, but can also have negative health consequences. This condition is often seen in achievement-oriented teenagers who seek to restrict their weight due to a fear of becoming obese. This condition can be a precursor to anorexia or bulimia if it is not detected and treated early.

Activity Nervosa

A condition in which the individual suffers from the ever-present compulsion to exercise, regardless of illness or injury. The desire to exercise excessively may result in poor performance in other areas of that individual's life due to the resulting fatigue, weakness, and unhealthy body weight.

Female Athlete Triad   In 1991, a team was formed by the American College of Sports Medicine to educate, initiate a change, and focus on the medical management of a triad of female disorders that included disordered eating, amenorrhea, and osteoporosis. A triangle is used to depict these disorders because each of the three are interlinked. Disordered eating behaviors result in weight loss and subsequent loss of body fat that halts menstruation. When amenorrhea occurs, calcium is lost and a decline

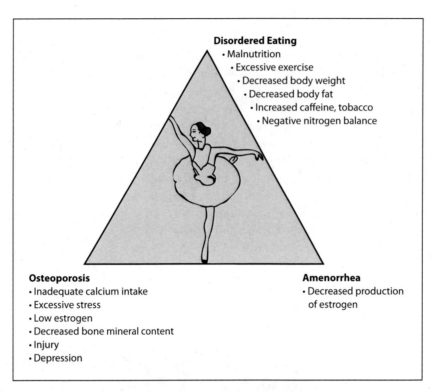

Figure 4.5   The Female Athlete Triad.

in bone mass occurs. This in turn causes osteoporosis and can easily result in stress fractures. Many times the inactivity necessary to allow stress fractures to heal causes depression that often leads an individual back into disordered eating behaviors, and the cycle continues.

Who Is at Risk?

By far, more women than men succumb to eating disorders; however, the incidence of eating disorders in men is believed to be very underreported.

It is estimated that one in every hundred teenage girls are anorexic. Anorexia usually occurs in adolescent women (90 percent of all reported cases), although all age groups can be affected. It is estimated that one in every five college-bound females is bulimic.

Individuals living in economically developed nations, such as the United States, are much more likely to suffer from an eating disorder, due to the dual factors of an abundance of available food and external, societal pressure. College campuses have a higher incidence of people with eating disorders, and upper-middle class women who are extremely self-critical are also more likely to become anorexic. Being aware of the groups at risk can be a large step toward prevention.

Activities such as dance and dance team, gymnastics, figure skating, track, and cheerleading tend to have higher instances of eating disorders. An estimate of people suffering from anorexia and bulimia within these populations is 15-60 percent. Male wrestlers and body builders are also at risk due to the unsafe practice of attempting to shed pounds quickly in an attempt to "make weight" before a competition.

Guidelines for Helping a Friend with an Eating Disorder

DO:
- listen with understanding
- appreciate the openness and trust in sharing with you his/her distress
- share your own struggles, be open and real
- learn more about eating disorders
- give support and be available
- give hope that with help and with patience he/she can free themselves from this disorder
- give your friend a list of resources for help

DO NOT:
- tell your friend he/she is crazy
- blame him/her
- gossip about your friend
- follow him/her around to check their eating or purging behavior
- ignore your friend
- reject him/her
- tell him/her to quit this ridiculous behavior
- feel compelled to solve their problem
- make excess comments about being thin

DO heed the signs.   Anorexic behavior includes extreme weight loss (often emaciation), obsessive dieting, and distorted body perception (a thin person thinks he/she is fat when they are not). Clues of bulimia are more subtle. Your friend may eat a great deal of food, then rush to the bathroom. She/he may hide laxatives or speak outright about the "magic method" of having the cake and not gaining weight. Anorexics and bulimics tend to be preoccupied with food and many have specific rituals tied to their eating patterns.

DO approach your friend gently, but persistently. Explain that you're worried; listen sympathetically. Don't expect your friend to admit he/she has a problem right away. The first step is realizing there is a problem; therefore, it is important to help your friend realize this.

DO focus on unhappiness as the reason your friend could benefit from help.   Point out how anxious or unhappy he/she has been lately, and emphasize that it does not have to be that way.

DO be supportive, but do not try to analyze or interpret their problem.   Being supportive is the most important thing you can do. Show your friend you believe in him/her—it will make a difference in recovery.

DO talk to someone about your own emotions if you feel the need.   An objective outsider can emphasize the fact that you are not responsible for your friend; you can only try to help that person help him/herself.

DO be yourself.   Be honest in sharing your feelings: i.e., "It's hard for me to watch you destroy yourself."

DO give non-judgmental feedback.   For example, "We haven't gone to lunch together in a while, is something wrong?" instead of "You haven't gone to eat with me in a while, do you have a problem?"

DO cooperate with your friend if he/she asks you to keep certain foods out of common storage areas. This may help prevent a binge on such foods.

DON'T keep the "secret"   from the family when your friend's health and thinking are impaired.

DON'T forget that denial   is a form of selective "deafness."

DON'T be deceived   by the excuse: "It's not really bad. I can control myself."

DON'T focus on your friend's weight or appearance. Focus on your concern about his/her health and well-being.

DON'T change your eating habits   when you're around your friend. Your "normal" eating is an example to your friend of a more healthy relationship with food.

Causes of Eating Disorders

The causes of anorexia and bulimia are numerous and complex. Cultural factors, family pressure, psychological factors, emotional disorders, and chemical imbalances can all contribute to eating disorders.

Forty to eighty percent of anorexics suffer from depression, as reduced levels of chemical neurotransmitters in the brain have been found in victims suffering from both eating disorders and depression. Links between hunger and depression have been discovered through research, which contributes to the depression a person with an eating disorder may feel.

For some bulimics, seasonality can adversely affect them, causing the disorder to worsen during the dark, winter months. Another startling statistic is that the onset of anorexia appears to peak in May, which is also the peak month for suicides.

Family factors are also critical. One study showed that 40 percent of all nine- to ten-year-old girls were trying to lose weight, many at the encouragement of their mothers. Mothers of anorexics are often over-involved in their child's life, while bulimic's mothers are many times critical and detached.

It is clear that many people who suffer from eating disorders do not have a healthy body image. From an early age, there is enormous pressure in our culture from society, family, friends, the media, and often from one's self to achieve the unachievable and unnecessary "perfect" body. A woman's self-worth is too often associated with other people's opinions, which in many cases put unrealistic emphasis on physical attractiveness.

Ways to Help

The best course of action for a person who suspects they know someone with an eating disorder is to be patient, supportive, and not judge the individual. Learn what you can about the problem by consulting an eating disorder clinic or counseling center (common on college campuses), and offer to help the ill person seek professional help.

Often, individuals suffering from an eating disorder do not realize or will not admit that they are ill. For this reason, seeking help or continuing/completing treatment for the disorder is often difficult.

Medical treatment is often necessary for eating disorders. However, it is extremely encouraging to note that eating disorders can be treated and a healthy weight and relationship with food can be restored. Because of the complexity of eating disorders, the best and most successful treatment is usually a combination of counseling, family therapy, cognitive behavior therapy, nutritional therapy, support groups, and drug therapy. Treatment, many times, includes a hospital stay and is usually resisted by the patient. Support for the anorexic or bulimic person by friends and family and the realization of the severity of the problem is critical to successful treatment of the illness.

REFERENCES

Donatelle, R.J. & Davis, L.G. *Access to Health* 4th ed., Allyn and Bacon, Boston, 1996.

Floyd, P.A., Mimms, S.E., and Yelding-Howard, C. *Personal Health: Perspectives & Lifestyles* 2nd ed., Morton Publishing Company, Englewood, CO, 1998.

Hales, Dianne. *An Invitation to Health* 8th ed., Brooks/Cole Publishing Company, New York, 1999.

Hoeger, W., and Hoeger, S.A. *Principle and Labs for Fitness and Wellness* 5th ed., Morton Publishing Company, Englewood, CO, 1999.

Hoeger, W.W.K. and Hoeger, S.A. *Lifetime Physical Fitness and Wellness: A Personalized Program* 8th ed., Thomson Wadsworth, Belmont,CA, 2005.

Hyman, B., Oden, G., Bacharach, D. & Collins, R. *Fitness for Living* 1st ed., Kendall/Hunt Publishing Company, Dubuque, Iowa, 1999.

Peterson, M.S. *Eat to Compete,* 2nd ed., Mosby, St. Louis, MO 63146.

Powers, S.K. & Todd, S.L. *Total Fitness and Wellness* 3rd ed., Allyn and Bacon, Boston, 2003.

Prentice, W., E. *Fitness and Wellness for Life* 6th ed., WCB McGraw-Hill, New York, 1999.

Pruitt, B.E. & Stein, J. *HealthStyles* 2nd ed., Allyn and Bacon, Boston, 1999.

Robbins, G., Powers, D., and Burgess, S. *A Wellness Way of Life* 4th ed., WCB McGraw-Hill, New York, 1999.

Rosato, F. *Fitness for Wellness* 3rd ed., West, Minneapolis, 1994.

Roth, G. *Why Weight? A Guide to Compulsive Eating,* Penguin Group, New York, 1999.

Student Health Services, Health Education, Texas A&M University. *FadDiets: Promises or Profit?,* 2002.

Student Health Services, Health Education, Texas A&M University. *Guidelines for Helping a Friend with an Eating Disorder,* 2002.

Webmaster@noah.cuny.edu

http://www.cfsan.fda.gov/~dms/transfat.html

http://www.ganesa.com/food/foodpyramid.gif

http://www.healthdepot.com

http://www.health.gov/dietaryguidelines/dga2000.htm

http://www.health.gov/dietaryguidelines/dga2000/document/aim.htm

http://www.health.gov/dietaryguidelines/dga2000/document/choose.htm

http://www.health.gov/dietaryguidelines/dga2005/document/html/executivesummary.htm

http://www.health.gov/dietaryguidelines/dga2005/document/html/chapter1.htm

http://www.nhlbi.nih.gov/health/public/heart/obesity/lose_wt/dine_out.htm

http://www.nhlbi.nih.gov/health/public/heart/obesity/lose_wt/shop.htm

http://www.nimh.nih.gov/publicat/eatingdisorder.cfm

http://vm.cfsan.fda.gov/~dms/foodlab.html

http://www.ers.usda.gov/AmberWaves/June05/Features/Will2005WholeGrain.htm

CONTACTS

American Dietetic Association
Get Nutrition Fact Sheets at
American Dietetic Association
Consumer Education Team
216 West Jackson Boulevard
Chicago, IL 60606
(send a self-addressed, stamped envelope), call 800–877–1600, ext. 5000 for other publications or 800–366–1655 for recorded food/nutrition messages.

American Obesity Association
1250 24th Street, NW, Suite 300
Washington, D.C. 20037
800–98–OBESE
Department of Nutrition Sciences
University of Alabama at Birmingham
Birmingham, AL 35294

Calorieking.com

Fitday.com

http://www.caloriesperhour.com/index_food.html
(Bounds et al)

CHAPTER 5

Exercises

LEGS

BACK SQUAT

Starting Position: Stand erect with the feet about shoulder width apart. The toes are pointed slightly out. Place the bar behind the neck and across the shoulders. Keep the head up and the back straight. Think about pointing your big toe at the ceiling.

Action: Spread the chest and lock the lower back. The downward movement is started by bending at the hips and sticking out the gluteal area. (Think of sitting in a chair.) Lower the body until the thighs are parallel with the floor. Knees should be pointing the same direction as the toes. Return to the starting position.

Precautions: Have partners assist as spotters during the exercise. Keep back straight and chest high throughout the movement. Rounding the back can place stress on spine and cause injury. Do not bounce at the bottom of the squat. Ideally, the knees won't travel in front of the toes.

NOTE: This exercise can be performed to any selected joint angle of the legs depending on the needs of the person training.

LUNGE

Starting Position: Stand erect with the feet about shoulder width apart. If using a barbell, place it behind the neck and across the shoulders. If using dumbbells, keep them at your sides. Keep the head up and the back straight.

Action: Step forward with the right leg and lower the body until the left knee is about three or four inches from the floor. Explosively push back to the starting position. Repeat the same action with the left leg, and return to the starting position.

Precautions: Keep the back straight and the head up during the movement. Do not bounce at the bottom part of the exercise. Do not let your front knee travel past the front toe.

FULL BODY

DEAD LIFT

Starting Position: Stand next to the bar with the front of legs touching the bar and the feet shoulder width apart. Bend down and grasp the bar with the palms facing toward the legs (or palms alternating front and back) and the hands about shoulder width apart. Bend the legs with the hips lowered and head up. Keep the natural arch in the back to take stress off the lower back.

Action: Pull the bar up along the legs until the body is upright and the bar is on the front of the thighs. Then return to the starting position.

Precautions: Keep the bar close to the legs to reduce back strain. Always keep the head up and lift with the legs.

CHEST

BARBELL BENCH PRESS

Starting Position:　Lie flat on the bench with the knees bent and feet flat on the floor. Use a palms-up grip, approximately the width of the shoulders. Hold the bar in a chest-rest position across the base of the pectorals (nipple line.) Keep the elbows at approximately 45° angle to the torso.

Action:　Press the bar directly upward until elbows lock, and then return to the starting position.

Precautions:　Do not arch the back or raise the buttocks during movement. Do not bounce the weight off the chest.

NOTE:　This exercise can be done using a narrow grip to increase resistance to the triceps.

BARBELL INCLINE BENCH PRESS

Starting Position: Sit on inclined bench with feet flat against the floor. Use a palms-up grip, approximately the width of the shoulders. Hold the bar in a chest-rest position (higher on the chest than flat bench press.)

Action: Press the bar upward until elbows lock, and then return to the starting position.

Precautions: Do not arch the back or raise the buttocks during movement. Do not bounce weight off the chest.

SHOULDERS

OVERHEAD PRESS

Starting Position: Can be done seated or standing, with a barbell or dumbbells. Use a palms-up grip with the bar placed at the top of the chest. The head is up and the back straight.

Action: Push the bar overhead until the arms are fully extended. Return to the starting position.

Precautions: Do not jerk the weight or use any unnecessary body motion in the movement. If standing, do not use the legs to start the movement.

DUMBBELL BENT-OVER ROWING

Starting Position: Start in a bent-over position with the upper torso parallel to the floor. The outside foot is on the floor with the knee slightly bent. Grasp the dumbbell with the arm fully extended, the opposite arm and leg supporting the body by contacting a bench for stability.

Action: Pull the dumbbell upward until it touches the torso, and then return to the starting position.

Precautions: Keep the elbow close to the body while doing the exercise. Do not jerk the weight or raise the body to assist in the movement.

UPPER BACK

LAT PULL-DOWN

Starting Position: Start in a seated position. Grasp the bar in a wide, palms-down grip with the arms fully extended. Lean back slightly and then maintain the angle at the hips.

Action: Pull the bar down until the bar is in front of the upper chest pinching the shoulder blades together in the back and then return to the starting position.

Precautions: Keep the upper body straight while maintaining the elected start angle. Do not jerk or raise the body to assist in the movement.

Credits

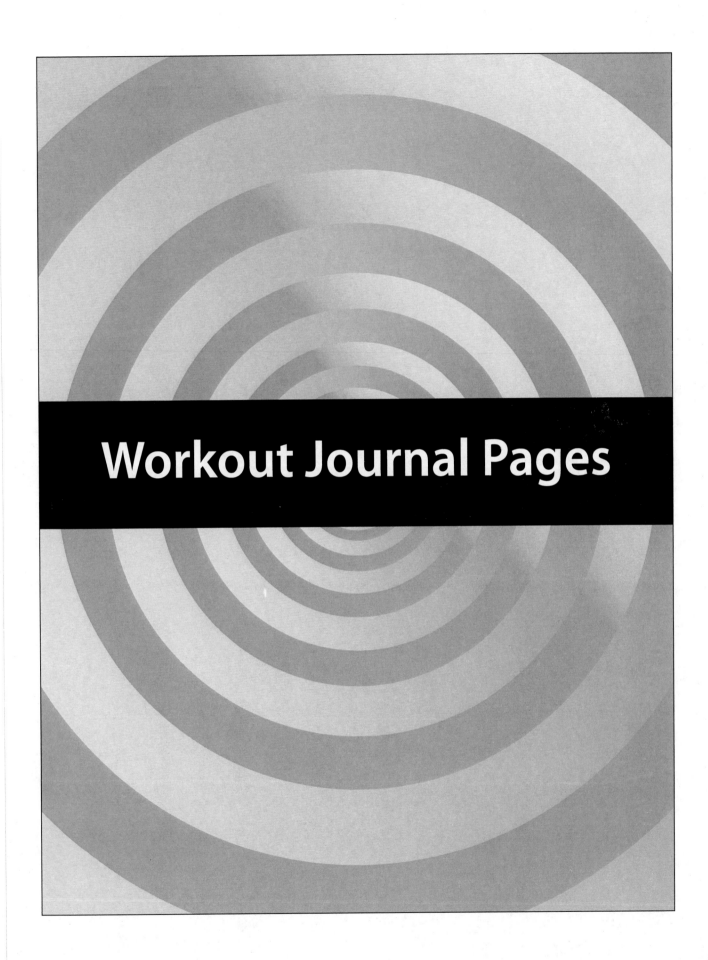

Workout Journal Pages

Date 9/5 Weekday TH **Name of Exercise** **(in the order that they are done)**	Wt	#reps	#sets	**Comments to self:** **Too light/heavy, Spotter** **helped me on . . .**
Example: Squats	115	10		Warm up set
	185	10	3	Target sets; heavy but do-able
Bench	~~85~~ 45	10	1	
~~Bench~~	85	10	2	
Squat	~~65~~ 45	10	1	
	85	10	1	
	105	10	1	
Abs				
· Planks	--	1 min		
· Twists	10	100	·	
· Oblique w/ weight	~~70~~ 25	10		

Date 7/10 Weekday T				Comments to self: Too light/heavy, Spotter helped me on . . .
Name of Exercise (in the order that they are done)	**Wt**	**#reps**	**#sets**	
SQUAT	45	10	1	
	95	10	1	
	135	10	2	
Bench	95	10	1	
	105	10	1	
	115	10	1	
DB Row	30	10 each side	1	
	25	10	2	
Overhead Press	30	10	1	
	50	10	1	
	40	10	1	
Step-ups	#N/A	10	1	

Date 9/12 Weekday TH Name of Exercise (in the order that they are done)	Wt	#reps	#sets	Comments to self: Too light/heavy, Spotter helped me on . . .
Overhead Press	45	10	1	
	55	10	2	
Squat Leg Press	90	10	1	
	110	10	1	
	140	10	2	
Bench	115	10	1	
	135	10	2	
Pull Downs	60	10	3	

Date 9/17 Weekday TU				Comments to self: Too light/heavy, Spotter helped me on . . .
Name of Exercise (in the order that they are done)	**Wt**	**#reps**	**#sets**	
Squat	85 95	10	1	
	135	10	1	
	155	10	1	
Bench	115	10	1	
	135	10	2	
Overhead	₹·45	10	1	
	55	10	1	
Row	25	10	2	
~~High Pull~~	45	10	2	
	70	10	1	

Date 9/19 Weekday TH				Comments to self: Too light/heavy, Spotter helped me on . . .
Name of Exercise (in the order that they are done)	Wt	#reps	#sets	
Squat (85%)	135	10	3	
Overhead (85%)	55	10	3	
Pulldowns	60	10	3	
High Pull	45	10	2	
	70	10	1	
Bench (100%)	135	10	3	

Date 9/24 Weekday TU **Name of Exercise** (in the order that they are done)	Wt	#reps	#sets	**Comments to self:** **Too light/heavy, Spotter** **helped me on . . .**
Squat	95	10	1	
B	155	10	3	
Bench	95	10	1	
	135	10	3	
Overhead	45	10	1	
	55	10	2	
Rows	25	10	4	
Abs				

Date 9/26 Weekday THURS. Name of Exercise (in the order that they are done)	Wt	#reps	#sets	Comments to self: Too light/heavy, Spotter helped me on . . .
Squat	115	10	1	
	165	10	3	
Bench	95	10	1	
	145	10	3	BARELY got the last set
~~Overhead~~	55	10	3	
Overhead	45	10	1	
	55	10	2	
Standing Pullovers	35	10	1	
	40	10	3	
Bicep Curls	15	10	3	
Rows	27.5	10	3	

Date 10/1 Weekday TU				Comments to self: Too light/heavy, Spotter helped me on . . .
Name of Exercise (in the order that they are done)	Wt	#reps	#sets	
Squat	115	10	1	
	165	10	3	
Bench	95	10	1	
	125	10	3	
Overhead	55	10	3	
Standing Triceps	35 30	10	1	
	40	10	2	
Rows	25	10	3	
Biceps	20	10	3	
Shrugs	45	10	3	

Date 10/3 Weekday TH Name of Exercise (in the order that they are done)	Wt	#reps	#sets	Comments to self: Too light/heavy, Spotter helped me on . . .
Squat	115	10	1	
	140	10	3	
Overhead	55	10	3	
High Pull	85	6	3	
Bench	105	10	1	
	145	10	3	

Date 10/8 Weekday TU **Name of Exercise** **(in the order that they are done)**	Wt	#reps	#sets	**Comments to self:** **Too light/heavy, Spotter** **helped me on . . .**
Row	25	10	4	
Squat	125	10	1	
	165	10	3	
Bench	95	10	1	
	135	10	3	
Overhead	55	10	3	
Triceps	30	10		
~~Brows~~	30	10	3	

Date 10/10 Weekday TH Name of Exercise (in the order that they are done)	Wt	#reps	#sets	Comments to self: Too light/heavy, Spotter helped me on . . .
Leg Press	90	10	4	
High Pull	85	6	3	
Bench	115	10	1	
	145	10	3	
Rows	30	10	3	
Triceps Pullovers	45	10	3	
Bi Curls	15	10	3	

10/15/13

Date IO Weekday TU	Wt	#reps	#sets	Comments to self: Too light/heavy, Spotter helped me on . . .
Name of Exercise (in the order that they are done)				
Overhead	55	10	1	
	55	25	1	
Bench	115	10	1	
	125	10	3	
Squat	155	10	1	
	165	10	1	
	165	17	1	
Rows	25	10	3	
Pullovers	45	10	3	
Bi Curls	15	10	3	

Date 10/17 Weekday TH Name of Exercise (in the order that they are done)	Wt	#reps	#sets	Comments to self: Too light/heavy, Spotter helped me on . . .
Bench	115	10	1	
	145	10	1	
	145		1	
Squat	135	10	1	
	155	10	3	
High Pull	95	6⅔	3	
Bench	115	10	1	
	135	10	1	
	145	15	1	
Rows	30	10	3	
Overhead Press	55	10	1	
	60	10	2	
Curls	17.5	10	3	
Oblique w/ weights	30	10	3	

Date _____ Weekday _____ Name of Exercise (in the order that they are done)	Wt	#reps	#sets	Comments to self: Too light/heavy, Spotter helped me on . . .
Squat	135	10	1	
	175	5	1	
	185	5	1	
Bench	195	5	1	
Bench	115	10	1	
	155	5	1	
	165	5	2	
	135	10	1	
Overhead	70	5	1	
	95	5	3	
Dead lift	135	4	1	
	185	4	3	
	145	4	2	
Pullover	35	10	1	
Curls	17.5	10	3	
Shrugs	40	10	3	
Oil Rig Abs	40	10	3	
Belongs on 10/24/13				

Date 10/24 Weekday TH Name of Exercise (in the order that they are done)	Wt	#reps	#sets	Comments to self: Too light/heavy, Spotter helped me on . . .
Bench	115	10	1	
	155	10	1	
	165	10	2	
	135	10	1	

Switch with the previous Log!

NB B follows

Date _10/29_ Weekday _TU_ **Name of Exercise** (in the order that they are done)	Wt	#reps	#sets	**Comments to self:** **Too light/heavy, Spotter** **helped me on . . .**
Squat	135	10	1	
	185	5	3	
Bench	115	10	1	
	145	8	3	
Overhead	70	5	1	
	95	5	1	
	70	5	2	
Curls	17.5	10	3	
Shrugs	40	10	3	
Ab-oil rig	40	10	3	
Rows	27.5	10	3	

Missed

Date _____ Weekday _____ **Name of Exercise** **(in the order that they are done)**	Wt	#reps	#sets	**Comments to self:** **Too light/heavy, Spotter** **helped me on . . .**

Date 11/5 Weekday TU				Comments to self: Too light/heavy, Spotter helped me on . . .
Name of Exercise (in the order that they are done)	**Wt**	**#reps**	**#sets**	
Squat 155	~~135~~	10	1	
	175	5	3	
155	~~135~~	10	1	
Bench	125	10	1	
	145	5	1	
	155	5	2	
	135	10	1	
Overhead	80	5	1	
	85	5	2	
	60	10	1	
Row	25	10	3	
Curls	25	8	3	
Shrugs	40	10	3	
Oil-Rig	40	10	3	
fatt Lat Pulls	60	10	1	
	70	10	2	

Date 11/7 Weekday TH	Wt	#reps	#sets	Comments to self: Too light/heavy, Spotter helped me on . . .
Name of Exercise (in the order that they are done)				
Deadlift	135	5	1	
	205	5	2	
	215	5	1	
	135	5	1	
Bench	135	10	1	
	155	5	1	
	165	5	2	
	135	10	1	
Leg Press	180	12	1	
	230	8	1	
	~~320~~ 270	8	1	
	320	8	1	
Overhead Press	55	10	1	
	75	5	3	
	55	10	1	
Curls	25	~~8~~ 8	3	
Shrugs	40	10	3	
Ovl-Rig	40	10	~~2~~ 3	
Rows	25	10	3	
Lat Pull downs	70	10	1	
	60	10	1	

Date 11/11 Weekday TU Name of Exercise (in the order that they are done)	Wt	#reps	#sets	Comments to self: Too light/heavy, Spotter helped me on . . .
Leg Press	270	10	1	
	360	5	1	
	410	5	2	
	180	10	1	
Bench	135	10	1	
	145	10	1	
	155	10	1	
	165	10	1	
Overhead	60	10	1	
	85	10	3	
	50	10	1	
Biceps	25	10	3	
Oil-Rigs	40	10	3	
Shrugs	40	10	3	

| Date 11/14   Weekday TH

Name of Exercise
(in the order that they are done)	Wt	#reps	#sets	Comments to self: Too light/heavy, Spotter helped me on . . .
Squat	155	10	1	
	195	5	3	
	155	10	1	
Bench	135	10	1	
	155	5	2	
	165	5	1	
	135	10	1	
Overhead	50	10	1	
	75	5	3	
	50	10	1	
Oil Rig	45	10	3	
Shrug	45	10	3	
Bicep	25	10	3	

Date _____ Weekday _____ **Name of Exercise** **(in the order that they are done)**	**Wt**	**#reps**	**#sets**	**Comments to self:** **Too light/heavy, Spotter** **helped me on . . .**

Date 4/11/21 Weekday TH **Name of Exercise** **(in the order that they are done)**	**Wt**	**#reps**	**#sets**	**Comments to self:** **Too light/heavy, Spotter** **helped me on . . .**
Squat	155	10	1	
	~~215~~ 295	3	1	
	215	3	2	
	155	10	1	
Deadlift	135	6	1	
	225	3	3	
Bench	135	10	1	
	175	3	3	

26 NOV Dungeons

Date 11/26 Weekday TU				
Name of Exercise (in the order that they are done)	**Wt**	**#reps**	**#sets**	**Comments to self:** Too light/heavy, Spotter helped me on . . .

Sick

But

Still Present at Class

Date 12/3 Weekday TU **Name of Exercise** **(in the order that they are done)**	Wt	#reps	#sets	**Comments to self:** **Too light/heavy, Spotter** **helped me on . . .**
Squat	135	10	1	
	185	2	1	
	225	1	1	
	245	1	1	
	135	10	1	
Bench	135	10	1	
	155	10	1	
	135	10 +35	1	
Overhead Ben Overhead	55	10	3	
Curls	15	10	3	
Shrags	45	10	3	
Oil-rigs	45	10	3	
Rows	25	10	2	

Date _____ Weekday _____ **Name of Exercise** **(in the order that they are done)**	**Wt**	**#reps**	**#sets**	**Comments to self:** **Too light/heavy, Spotter** **helped me on . . .**

Date _____ Weekday _____ **Name of Exercise** **(in the order that they are done)**	**Wt**	**#reps**	**#sets**	**Comments to self:** **Too light/heavy, Spotter** **helped me on . . .**

Date ———— Weekday ———— **Name of Exercise** **(in the order that they are done)**	Wt	#reps	#sets	**Comments to self:** **Too light/heavy, Spotter** **helped me on . . .**

Date _____ Weekday _____ **Name of Exercise** **(in the order that they are done)**	**Wt**	**#reps**	**#sets**	**Comments to self:** **Too light/heavy, Spotter** **helped me on . . .**

Date _____ Weekday _____ **Name of Exercise** **(in the order that they are done)**	**Wt**	**#reps**	**#sets**	**Comments to self:** **Too light/heavy, Spotter** **helped me on . . .**

Date _____ Weekday _____ **Name of Exercise** **(in the order that they are done)**	**Wt**	**#reps**	**#sets**	**Comments to self:** **Too light/heavy, Spotter** **helped me on . . .**

Date _____ Weekday _____ **Name of Exercise** **(in the order that they are done)**	**Wt**	**#reps**	**#sets**	**Comments to self:** **Too light/heavy, Spotter** **helped me on . . .**

Date _____ Weekday _____ **Name of Exercise** **(in the order that they are done)**	Wt	#reps	#sets	**Comments to self:** **Too light/heavy, Spotter** **helped me on . . .**

Date _____ Weekday _____ **Name of Exercise** **(in the order that they are done)**	**Wt**	**#reps**	**#sets**	**Comments to self:** **Too light/heavy, Spotter** **helped me on . . .**

Date _____ Weekday _____ **Name of Exercise** **(in the order that they are done)**	**Wt**	**#reps**	**#sets**	**Comments to self:** **Too light/heavy, Spotter** **helped me on . . .**

Date _____ Weekday _____ **Name of Exercise** **(in the order that they are done)**	**Wt**	**#reps**	**#sets**	**Comments to self:** **Too light/heavy, Spotter** **helped me on . . .**

Date _____ Weekday _____ **Name of Exercise** **(in the order that they are done)**	**Wt**	**#reps**	**#sets**	**Comments to self:** **Too light/heavy, Spotter** **helped me on . . .**

Date _____ Weekday _____ Name of Exercise (in the order that they are done)	Wt	#reps	#sets	Comments to self: Too light/heavy, Spotter helped me on . . .

Date _____ Weekday _____ **Name of Exercise** **(in the order that they are done)**	**Wt**	**#reps**	**#sets**	**Comments to self:** **Too light/heavy, Spotter** **helped me on . . .**

Date _____ Weekday _____ **Name of Exercise** **(in the order that they are done)**	**Wt**	**#reps**	**#sets**	**Comments to self:** **Too light/heavy, Spotter** **helped me on . . .**

Date _____ Weekday _____ **Name of Exercise** **(in the order that they are done)**	**Wt**	**#reps**	**#sets**	**Comments to self:** **Too light/heavy, Spotter** **helped me on . . .**

Date _____ Weekday _____ Name of Exercise (in the order that they are done)	Wt	#reps	#sets	Comments to self: Too light/heavy, Spotter helped me on . . .

Date _____ Weekday _____ **Name of Exercise** **(in the order that they are done)**	**Wt**	**#reps**	**#sets**	**Comments to self:** **Too light/heavy, Spotter** **helped me on . . .**

Date _____ Weekday _____ Name of Exercise (in the order that they are done)	Wt	#reps	#sets	Comments to self: Too light/heavy, Spotter helped me on . . .

Date _____ Weekday _____ **Name of Exercise** **(in the order that they are done)**	Wt	#reps	#sets	**Comments to self:** **Too light/heavy, Spotter** **helped me on . . .**

Date _____ Weekday _____ **Name of Exercise** **(in the order that they are done)**	**Wt**	**#reps**	**#sets**	**Comments to self:** **Too light/heavy, Spotter** **helped me on . . .**

Date _____ Weekday _____ **Name of Exercise** **(in the order that they are done)**	Wt	#reps	#sets	**Comments to self:** **Too light/heavy, Spotter** **helped me on . . .**

Date _____ Weekday _____ **Name of Exercise** **(in the order that they are done)**	Wt	#reps	#sets	**Comments to self:** **Too light/heavy, Spotter** **helped me on . . .**

Date _____ Weekday _____ **Name of Exercise** **(in the order that they are done)**	**Wt**	**#reps**	**#sets**	**Comments to self:** **Too light/heavy, Spotter** **helped me on . . .**

Date _____ Weekday _____ **Name of Exercise** **(in the order that they are done)**	**Wt**	**#reps**	**#sets**	**Comments to self:** **Too light/heavy, Spotter** **helped me on . . .**

NOTES

NOTES

NOTES

NOTES

NOTES

NOTES

NOTES

NOTES

NOTES

Quiz Nov. 21 st

Protein Synthesis	Protein Breakdown
• Exercise	• Sedentary lifestyle
• Nutrition	• Mal-Nutrition
• Growth Hormone	

Δ

*Macro-Nutrition	*Micro-Nutrition
• CHO 4 Cal/g	- Vitamin
- Fat 9 Cal/g	- Mineral
- Protein 4 Cal/g	- Anti-oxidants
	- Water

*Body Composition   *Methods to measure body-composition

- Fat, Non-fat

- Fat, muscle, mineral, water